OSPREY MILITARY

CAMPAIGN SERIES   36

CANNAE 216 BC

SEKIGAHARA 1600

SEKIGAHARA 1600

ANTHONY J. BRYANT

First published in Great Britain in 1995 by
Osprey Publishing, Elms Court, Chapel Way,
Botley, Oxford OX2 9LP, United Kingdom

00 01 02 03 04 10 9 8 7 6 5 4 3 2 1

Also published as Campaign *40 Sekigahara 1600*

ISBN 1 84176 116 8

Military Editor: Lee Johnson.
Edited by Tony Holmes.
Designed by: the Black Spot

Bird's eye view illustrations by Peter Harper.
Cartography by Micromap.

Filmset in Great Britain.
Printed in China through World Print Ltd.

FOR A CATALOGUE OF ALL BOOKS PUBLISHED
BY OSPREY MILITARY AND AVIATION
PLEASE WRITE TO:

The Marketing Manager, Osprey Direct USA, PO
Box 130, Sterling Heights, MI 48311-0130, USA.
Email: info@ospreydirectusa.com

The Marketing Manager, Osprey Direct UK, PO
Box 140, Wellingborough, Northants,
NN8 4ZA, United Kingdom.
Email: info@ospreydirect.co.uk

VISIT OSPREY AT
www.ospreypublishing.com

DEDICATION

To Lillian and Chris Csernica, with eternal gratitude...

ACKNOWLEDGEMENTS

This book would not have been possible without the co-operation and assistance of the curators, clergy and managers of the museums, temples, shrines, castles and other institutions visited. Especially worthy of note is the management of the armour shop Yoroi no Kôzan-dô, Tokyo; the Sekigahara Museum; Sekigahara Warland; and the Katô Kiyomasa/Toyotomi Hideyoshi Memorial Hall, Nagoya.

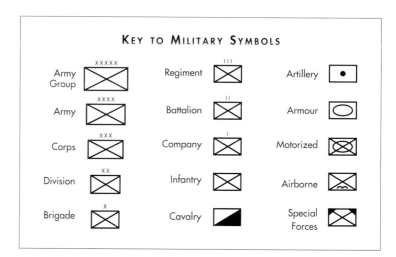

FRONT AND BACK COVERS: The Battle of Sekigahara (Courtesy of Stephen Turnbull)

CONTENTS

THE ORIGINS OF THE CAMPAIGN

Toyotomi Hideyoshi was dead. The great unifier had been able to do what few before him had done. He had taken a nation embroiled in intrigues and civil war, and one by one brought all the warring clans under his control.

Hideyoshi had begun his grand conquest by picking up the pieces of the hegemony of his own slain lord, Oda Nobunaga, claiming guardianship of the latter's young son, and starting to make alliances and expand his influence. His actions alienated many of Nobunaga's old vassals, and Hideyoshi was forced to make war on his erstwhile comrades; those who would not freely ally with him and acknowledge him as their lord felt the wrath of his army.

Even Tokugawa Ieyasu, one of the most powerful feudal lords in Japan, finally joined Hideyoshi's banner. Though Ieyasu might eventually have defeated Hideyoshi, he decided the more certain path was alliance — and patience.

Despite all the attempts of fawning contemporary biographers, who tried to tie him to the ancient Fujiwara clan, Hideyoshi had been born of peasant stock, and there was no way he could claim the title of shôgun. He had to settle for the office of kanpaku, a civil prime minister, but was, nevertheless, the undisputed master of Japan, and his word could be backed up with an army, just as any shôgun's would.

By the 1590s the ageing hegemon wanted an heir to succeed him, so in 1592 he transferred the position of kanpaku to his adopted son, Hidetsugu, and took for himself the title taikô (used by retired kanpaku), by which he is commonly known.

Japan was at peace for the first time in decades, and Hideyoshi — like Arthur in a too-successful Camelot — saw and felt the stirrings of his underlings for some military glory. His allies and vassals were battle-hardened veterans, and they had the egos and ambitions in keeping with their experiences.

Hideyoshi decided to launch a campaign to conquer China, with the intermediate goal of gaining control of Korea. As ambitious as the project was, it was met with considerable enthusiasm from most of his vassal lords. In 1592 a flotilla sailed to Korea with 130,000 samurai. The Japanese met with several initial successes, but when a Chinese army poured across the

LEFT *Toyotomi Hideyoshi (1536-1598), the great unifier, built an empire the stability of which he could not guarantee for his five-year-old heir. His death in 1598 left the nation under the control of two five-man councils that were unable — or unwilling — to cooperate to see the late unifier's wishes come true. Several of his foster sons would participate in the battle at Sekigahara, and one — Kobayakawa Hideaki — would betray his cause. (Nakamura Park, Nagoya)*

border to help the fleeing Korean king, the situation changed. Hideyoshi sent another 60,000 men to support their positions, and the stalemate began.

When a son, Hideyori, was born to the taikô in his fifty-seventh year (in 1593), relations soured with the kanpaku Hidetsugu – three years later, the deposed Hidetsugu was invited to commit seppuku, ritual disembowelment, for some perceived plot against his adoptive father and former sponsor.)

The problems at home distracted Hideyoshi from the Korean campaign, and he sent an embassy to China to discuss terms for peace. The embassy finally returned in 1596 with an unacceptable reply from the Chinese emperor. Hideyoshi was angered at this refusal, and even more upset that the Chinese emperor was willing merely to invest him with the title of 'King of Japan', which would make him, in essence, a vassal of the Chinese emperor (to say nothing of making him guilty of an act of lèse majesté against the reigning Japanese emperor, from whom Hideyoshi held his position).

The next year Hideyoshi responded by sending 100,000 more men to Korea under the command of his wife's nephew (another adopted son), Kobayakawa Hideaki, who was all of 15 years of age. Plagued by conflicting egos within and disease without, the expedition was doomed to failure.

In May 1598 Hideyoshi fell ill. Fearing for his son's safety (and anxious to protect his inheritance), the taikô called together his most powerful and wealthy vassals: Tokugawa Ieyasu, Maeda Toshiie, Uesugi Kagekatsu, Môri Terutomo and Ukita Hideie. None of them was worth less than a million koku a year. (One koku, a unit of measure representing approximately 180 litres of rice, was how wealth was measured in feudal Japan: it was the amount of rice believed necessary to keep a man alive for a year.) Hideyoshi made them swear to support the five-year-old Hideyori in his position, and to treat the boy as if he were Hideyoshi himself. To Maeda Toshiie and Tokugawa Ieyasu the taikô entrusted the care and raising of his son, though Toshiie would be the actual physical guardian. The lords agreed, and thus became the five tairô, a council of regents.

These regents were to work side by side with the five commissioners (bugyô) Hideyoshi had earlier appointed to oversee government of the capitol. Together they were to run the country in Hideyori's name until he came of age.

The taikô also ordered that the armies be recalled from Korea. This split his vassals into two camps, one camp thought victory could be taken, and didn't want to return, while the other was more than willing to quit the campaign. When those favouring withdrawal began to do so, the others had no choice but to follow, since their positions quickly became untenable.

This served to create enemies among the bugyô, for many would remember the withdrawal forced on them, and their resultant loss of face.

Then, on 15 September, 1598, Hideyoshi died.

In order to better protect his own interests, Ieyasu installed himself in Fushimi Castle, the late Hideyoshi's personal fortress, and was viewed by the other members of the council as a potential usurper. However true this

Oda Nobunaga (1534-1582) was long since dead, but it was his efforts at establishing unity that had set the stage for Hideyoshi to come to power. With Hideyoshi dead, a power vacuum had to be filled. This statue, on the grounds of Kiyosu Castle, shows the warlord in a full suit of densely laced armour. His assassin, Akechi Mitsuhide, was the father of Christian convert Hosokawa Gracia, the wife of Hosokawa Tadaoki, one of Ieyasu's most loyal general-retainers.

accusation may have been, Hideyori, at the age of five, was scarcely in a position to govern. Maeda Toshiie, in residence in Ôsaka Castle with Hideyori, grew concerned.

The tairô were bound by certain rules, one of them being that no marriages of their children were to be contracted for political reasons. In point of fact, it was simply impossible for a daimyô to marry off a son or daughter in that day and age without some political effect. Ieyasu, in particular, married several children to the sons and daughters of powerful men to seal alliances.

Ishida Mitsunari, one of the five bugyô and an inveterate schemer, had been moving behind the scenes to somehow lessen Ieyasu's influence or

One of the most severe of the 'conventional' helmet shapes was the akoda-nari. These helmets were common in the last half of the 16th century. (Yoroi no Kôzan-dô)

depose him altogether. He went to Ôsaka Castle to talk to the ageing and ailing Toshiie about Ieyasu, but Hosokawa Tadaoki, a friend of both Ieyasu and the Maeda clan, stepped in on the sly. Privately, Hosokawa pointed out to Maeda Toshinaga that his father, Toshiie, and Ieyasu were the two most powerful men of their age. Should Mitsunari succeed in somehow eliminating Ieyasu, that would leave as power broker only the ailing Toshiie, who was not long for this world; and Toshinaga, who was young, would have a great deal of trouble staying alive with people like Mitsunari around. It was simply in his interests to keep Ieyasu around. Toshinaga readily saw Tadaoki's point, and hurried to convince his father not to oppose Ieyasu.

This didn't stop the other regents from trying to call for Ieyasu's resignation, but he ignored them. His refusal to even discuss matters with them further strained relations, but there was nothing they could do short of declaring war, and there was as yet no need for such a drastic step. Besides, no one had sufficient power to stand up to the might of the Tokugawa, and there was yet no single figure who could lead a coalition against him.

The only option Mitsunari saw left to him was to have Ieyasu assassinated, but his plot failed, and when Ieyasu's generals heard about it, several of them (Katô Kiyomasa, Ikeda Terumasa, Asano Yukinaga, Katô Yoshiaki, Hosokawa Tadaoki and Kuroda Nagamasa) decided to eliminate Mitsunari instead. To escape their wrath, Mitsunari was forced to flee

THE PROVINCES OF JAPAN

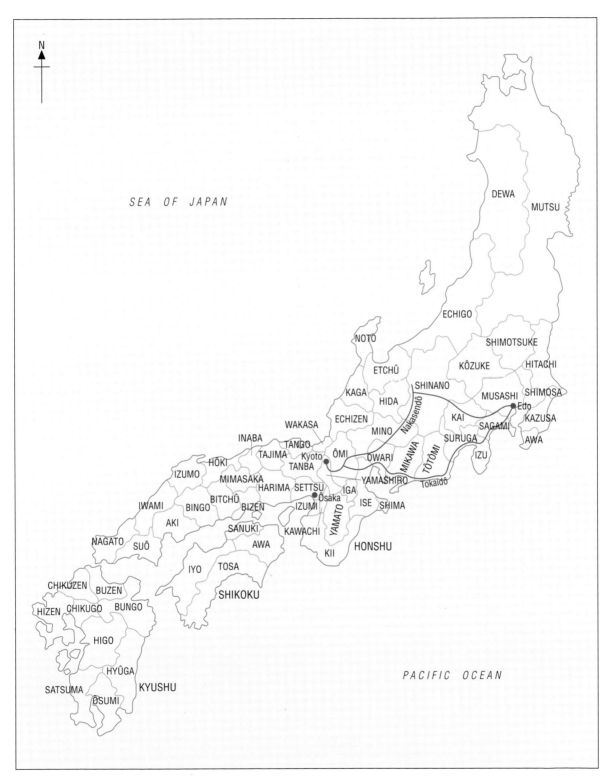

N

SEA OF JAPAN

DEWA
MUTSU

ECHIGO

NOTO
SHIMOTSUKE
KÔZUKE
HITACHI

ETCHÛ
SHINANO
MUSASHI SHIMOSA
KAGA
HIDA
Edo
KAI
KAZUSA
ECHIZEN
MINO
SAGAMI
AWA
WAKASA
Nakasendô
SURUGA
INABA
TANGO
ÔMI
OWARI
IZU
TAJIMA
Kyoto
MIKAWA
TÔTÔMI
HÔKI
TANBA
YAMASHIRO
Tokaidô
IZUMO
MIMASAKA
HARIMA SETTSU
IGA
ISE
SHIMA
IWAMI
BITCHÛ
Ôsaka
BINGO
BIZEN
IZUMI
YAMATO
AKI
KAWACHI
NAGATO
SANUKI
HONSHU
SUÔ
AWA
KII
IYO
TOSA
CHIKUZEN
SHIKOKU
BUZEN
HIZEN CHIKUGO BUNGO

HIGO

HYÛGA
KYUSHU
SATSUMA
ÔSUMI

PACIFIC OCEAN

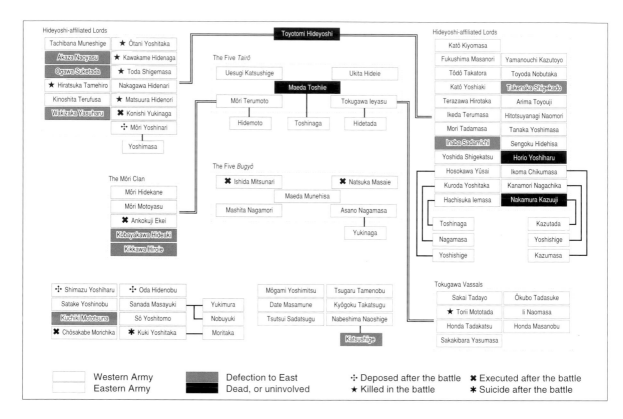

Ôsaka Castle at night dressed as a woman and riding in a lady's palanquin. His choice of destination was both baffling and unexpected, Fushimi Castle, and Ieyasu.

Mitsunari begged Ieyasu for protection and, oddly enough, Ieyasu consented to shelter him. Some historians have wondered how Ieyasu could have done something so outwardly dangerous and foolish; others speculate that Ieyasu could see right through Mitsunari, and so reasoned that a living enemy he could predict was better than a dead one with a possible new threat elsewhere. To put him out of the way, Ieyasu ordered Mitsunari to return home to his own fief, in Sawayama Castle, in the spring of 1599 under the watchful eye of Hideyasu, Ieyasu's son.

The venerable Maeda Toshiie died that same spring, but not before Hosokawa Tadaoki had been able to win one of Toshiie's sons (Toshinaga, the heir) and most of his vassals solidly over to Ieyasu's 'side'. With the passing of Toshiie, the position of physical guardian of Hideyori was suddenly vacant, so Ieyasu promptly assumed that rôle, and moved into Ôsaka Castle, making it his own (an action that only served to further anger the commissioners and the remaining regents).

On 22 August, while Ieyasu was preoccupied organising a campaign to deal with a rebellious lord, Uesugi Kagekatsu, in the north, Mitsunari acted. He and a quorum of the five bugyô and three of the other four tairô (there was one abstention, Toshinaga had assumed his late father's position, but he remained silent when it came to censuring Ieyasu) issued a formal complaint to Ieyasu, making 13 charges against him. Among them were

This chart shows the major daimyô involved in the battle, and how they were related to the old hegemony of Hideyoshi. (Some of those fighting were actually the sons or brothers of those indicated here.) A chart showing their familial relations would look like a spiders web, with sons of one marrying daughters of another back and forth across lines. Few of the politically minded marriages would have affected who fought on which side. Personal loyalties would outweigh family ties for many.

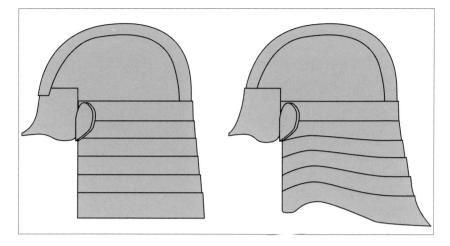

The three-plate helmet was produced principally by two schools. On the left is the Etchû kabuto; on the right is the Hineno kabuto. Note the differences: the central plate ends under the visor in the Hineno school, and over it in the Etchû model. The shikoro is also different. With its narrow profile and reduced bulk and weight, the Hineno-jikoro became the standard for many different styles of helmet.

condemnations of the political marriages Ieyasu had arranged, and the fact that he had taken up residence in Hideyoshi's castle as if it were his own. That the charges were essentially all true is academic; Ieyasu took this as an out-and-out declaration of war. Also academic is whether this had been the intent of the anti-Tokugawa coalition. Should they have seen the response their action would elicit; would they have gone ahead, knowing Ieyasu would declare war? One can only speculate.

Political camps had long-since formed, and virtually all the daimyô in Japan aligned one way or the other, behind the Toyotomi loyalists under Ishida Mitsunari (soon to become what is now called the Western Army), or under Tokugawa Ieyasu (the Eastern Army).

Both sides began laying secret plans in earnest, for it would only be a matter of time before open hostilities broke out. In just a few more months, the final struggle for power would take place near a small village, in a narrow valley, between several mountain ranges, called Sekigahara.

THE COMMANDERS

THE EASTERN ARMY

Tokugawa Ieyasu (1542–1616), lord of the Kantô plain (modern-day Tokyo and environs), was a descendant of the great Minamoto clan. The Minamoto gave Japan such luminaries as Yoshitsune, Yoritomo and Yoshiie. They became the only family from which the shôgun could come. The Minamoto themselves were long gone by 1600, but many branch families existed, and the Tokugawa were pre-eminent among them.

Ieyasu was the wealthiest daimyô in Japan. He ruled all eight provinces making up the Kantô, Japan's 'breadbasket'; domains that yielded him a total of 2.5 million koku, more than twice that of his nearest rival. With this wealth came influence and power. His armies were the largest, his men the best trained, his friends the most loyal. As a member of the tairô, Ieyasu also had a veneer of authority as a legacy from the late taikô.

When Hideyoshi had ordered the Korean invasion, the Kyûshu and Shikoku daimyô had borne the brunt of the cost in men and matériel, and Ieyasu, safe in the Kantô, had been shrewd enough to avoid any direct involvement in the campaign; while many of his enemies (and allies) had gone to fight, he had remained completely untouched by the conflict, his armies intact and in Japan.

He had missed several opportunities to gain dominance over the nation, dating back to Nobunaga's assassination. Having been caught in the wrong place when Nobunaga was killed, he had valiantly risked his life racing across the country through hostile territory to attempt to avenge Nobunaga; but Hideyoshi was already there, so it was he, not Ieyasu, who was able to gain the popular support as the man who had put down the dastardly assassin Akechi Mitsuhide.

Always patient, he had bided his time; his chance would come. There is an old story that has Nobunaga as the man kneading the rice cakes, Hideyoshi as the man cooking them, and Ieyasu as the man who gets to eat them in the end.

It is an apt analogy. Nobunaga had never conquered all of Japan, but he might have. He definitely set the stage for Hideyoshi to come in and finish subduing the nation. Under Hideyoshi, however, there were still egos – powerful, hostile, well-armed egos – at work. It was up to Ieyasu to bring them all under his control and restore order. The bakufu (the shô-

Tokugawa Ieyasu (1542-1616) may have been the best general and strategist in Japanese history. At the very least, he was incredibly gifted, and almost always seemed to be in the right place at the right time. He was also phenomenally wealthy and powerful, and able to command great loyalty from friends and vassals alike.
(Katô Kiyomasa/ Toyotomi Hideyoshi Museum)

In contrast to the Western Army, the Eastern Army had more commanders of name who were unswervingly loyal to their cause. The crests of some of those commanders are shown here. Top row, left to right: Tokugawa, Hosokawa, Honda, Kyôgoku. Middle row: Ikeda, Fukushima, Yamanouchi, Kuroda. Bottom row: Ii, Tôdô, Hachisuka, Ikoma.

Katô Kiyomasa (1562-1611) was in Kyûshu during the campaign, fighting partly on Ieyasu's behalf and partly on his own. His ferocity in Hideyoshi's Korean campaigns had earned him the title 'Kisho-kan' or 'devil general.' Though a Toyotomi loyalist at heart, Kiyomasa fought on the side of Ieyasu for several reasons, not the least of which was his great hatred of Ishida Mitsunari. Ieyasu is commonly believed to have had a hand in Kiyomasa's death years later, fearing that the latter might back Hideyoshi's heir. (Katô Shrine, Nakamura Park, Nagoya)

gunal government) had been non-existent for nearly 30 years, and few were alive who remembered it when it had been fully functional, still decades earlier. Ieyasu saw it as his destiny – as a son of the Minamoto – to restore the bakufu.

He was a veteran commander, 58 years of age, with perhaps as many as 50 battles under his belt. He had been able to make alliances through diplomacy and marriage with many of the more powerful daimyô, and the time was right for action.

Fighting under the banner of Tokugawa Ieyasu were many experienced battlelords.

Katô Kiyomasa (1562–1611), aged 38, was a valiant general who had earned a name for himself in the Korean campaign. As a close friend of Hideyoshi (indeed, they had been born a few hundred yards – though several years – apart, and their mothers were supposedly related), Kiyomasa owed a great deal to the taikô's favour. It was a shock to his friends when he came out for Ieyasu against the Toyotomi loyalists. His allegiance was more a reflection of his hatred of Mitsunari who had more than once impugned and injured Kiyomasa's honour in Korea.

Kiyomasa was a devout member of the Nichiren Buddhist sect (the only sect of Buddhism in Japan that can be called hostile to outsiders), and he hated Christians with a passion. That he shared the Kyûshu province of Higo with the Christian daimyô Konishi Yukinaga (each held half as his fief) galled him no end. During the Sekigahara campaign, Kiyomasa did not participate in the main battle; rather, he stayed in Kyûshu, where he helped put down uprisings of loyalist forces, notably in actions involving attacks on Yukinaga's castles.

Katô Yoshiaki (1563–1631), no relation of Katô Kiyomasa, had also served in Korea, and was also originally a vassal of Hideyoshi's. After the latter's death, Yoshiaki had allied himself with Kiyomasa and Fukushima Masanori as the military force against Mitsunari and his political machine. His fief was a large part of Iyo, on northern Shikoku.

ABOVE *The simple three-plate zu-nari kabuto was often dressed up to make it more individualised. This variation is called an Ichi-no-Tani kabuto, and the sloping panel is intended to evoke the image of the cliff-face Minamoto no Yoshitsune led a charge down during the Genpei War (1180-1183). Both Ieyasu and Kuroda Nagamasa had helmets that were variants of this basic pattern. (Gifu Castle)*

LEFT *Ii Naomasa led a corps of warriors all clad in red lacquered armour. They came to be called 'Ii's Red Devils.' This modern reproduction is of Naomasa's own armour, a style called hishinui-dô, after the cross-lace 'rivets'. The large horns were gilt. (Yoroi no Kôzan-dô)*

Kuroda Nagamasa (1568–1623), aged 32, had also served in Korea, and before that in Kyûshu during the final stages of Hideyoshi's unification of the nation. Nagamasa was a Christian, albeit a lukewarm one, and as a child had been baptised with the name Damian.

One of the most recognisable units in the campaign was the 3,600-man contingent of Ii Naomasa (1561–1602). Naomasa, aged 40, understood the value of psychology, and so had every one of his samurai wear red-lacquered armour, regardless of the actual type. So ferocious did they appear – and perform, it would seem – that they were nicknamed 'Ii no akazonae', or 'Ii's Red Devils'. His fief, held from Ieyasu, was Takasaki.

THE WESTERN ARMY

Ishida Mitsunari (1560–1600), the de facto commander-in-chief of the loyalist forces, was descended from the Fujiwara, an ancient aristocratic family that had once controlled the empire's civil government. He was, however, a poor relation, and could boast neither the influence nor wealth of Ieyasu.

He was one of the five bugyô, or administrators, named by Hideyoshi in 1585 to govern Kyôto (the other four were Maeda Munehisa, Natsuka Masaie, Asano Nagamasa and Mashita Nagamori), a position in which he seems to have performed well.

Mitsunari was devoted to Hideyoshi – some would use the term 'lapdog' – and, after the death of the latter, to his son Hideyori. At least, he appeared to be devoted to Hideyori. Allegations have been levelled from time to time – and they carry considerable weight – that Mitsunari's real motives were less than honourable. Whether his intent was honestly to secure Hideyori's right to rule, or merely to advance his own position, we may never know.

Regardless of his motives, Mitsunari was an inveterate schemer; and what he couldn't accomplish through diplomacy he was more than willing to accomplish by less acceptable means. At least once he tried to have Ieyasu assassinated, and his ruthless rounding up of hostages led to the brutal death of Hosokawa Gracia, wife of one of Ieyasu's generals.

Oddly, Mitsunari owed his position and rank not so much to his martial prowess or family ties as to his skills at preparing and serving tea. The tea ceremony was a major cult in the military aristocracy, and the taikô had enthusiastically endorsed it and encouraged its growth. Hideyoshi was supposedly so taken by Mitsunari's precision and artistry with the ceremony that he immediately adopted him into his inner circle, where Mitsunari displayed his administrative gifts and rose to be (arguably) the pre-eminent figure in the great unifier's administrative staff.

His personal fief, held from Hideyoshi, was the province of Ômi, in the centre of the waist of Honshû. His seat was Sawayama Castle, which was strategically sited on the Nakasendô, a great trunk road running through the heart of Honshû, and played a major part in the battle's main conflict.

Mitsunari had served with no special distinction in the Korean campaign as a member of Ukita Hideie's staff. He was considered by many,

Ishida Mitsunari (1560-1600) was an able administrator, but he lacked foresight. His greatest skill was intrigue, but his personality defects undermined the success of this intrigue in the long run. His brusque manner had also created many enemies for him, many of whom chose to fight on the side of the East not out of great loyalty for Ieyasu, but out of a desire to wreak vengeance on a man many considered a civilian interloper. From a contemporary portrait.

THE ALLIANCES: JAPAN IN SEPTEMBER 1600

—Mutsu and Echigo—
1. Tsugaru Tamenobu
2. Nanbu Toshinao
3. Date Masamune
4. Sôma Yoshitoshi
5. Katakura Kagenaga
6. *Iwaki Sadataka*
7. & 15. *Uesugi Kagekatsu*

—Dewa—
8. Akita Sanesue
9. Tozawa Masamori
10. *Onoji Yoshimichi*
11. Môgami Yoshiakira

—Echigo—
12. Murakami Yoshiaki
13. Mizoguchi Hidekatsu
14. Hori Hidenori

—Shimotsuke—
16. Ôzeki Sukemasu
17. Ôdawara Harusumi
18. Nasu Sukeharu
19. Gamô Hideyuki
20. Narita Yasuchika
21. –unknown–
22. Sano Masatsuna

—Hitachi—
23. *Satake Yoshinobu*

—Shimôsa—
24. Yûki Hideyasu

—Ueno—
25. Sanada Nobuyuki

—Kantô provinces—
26. Tokugawa Ieyasu

—Awa—
27. Satomi Yoshiyasu

—Shinano—
28. Minagawa Shigemura
29. Sakuma Yasumasa
30. Mori Tadamasa

31. *Sanada Masayuki*
32. Sengoku Hidehisa
33. Hineno Yoshiaki
34. Ishikawa Yasunaga
35. –unknown–
36. Kyôgoku Takatomo

—Kai—
37. Asano Yukinaga

—Suruga—
38. Nakamura Ujitsugu
39. Nakamura Kazuuji

—Tôtômi—
40. Yamanouchi Kazutoyo
41. Arima Toyouji
42. Matsushima Shigetsune
43. Horio Tadauji

—Nôtô, Etchû, Kaga—
44. Maeda Toshinaga
45. *Maeda Toshimasa*

—Hida—
46. Kanamori Nagachika

—Mikawa—
47. Ikeda Terumasa
48. Tanaka Yoshimasa
49. Mizuno Katsunari

—Owari—
50. Fukushima Masanori
51. Hitotsuyanagi Naomori
52. *Ishikawa Sadaharu*

—Mino—
53. Kawajiri Naotsugu
54. Tamura Tadamasa
55. Oda Hidenobu
56. Inaba Sadamichi ****
57. Katô Sadayasu ****
58. *Marumo Chikayoshi*
59. Tokunaga Toshimasa
60. Nishio Mitsuyuki
61. *Itô Morimasa*
62. Ichibashi Nagakatsu

63. Takagi Morikane

—Echizen—
64. Tanba Nagashige
65. Yamaguchi Munenaga
66. Aoyama Munekatsu
67. Aoyama Kazunori
68. Tanba Nagamasa
69. Ôtani Yoshitsugu
70. Oda Hideo
(Others in Echizen:
Akaza Naoyasu, ****
Teranishi Haruyuki,
Toda Shigemasa, etc.)

—Wakasa—
71. *Kinoshita Katsutoshi*
72. Kinoshita Toshifusa

—Ômi—
73. Ishida Mitsunari
74. Kuchiki Mototsune ****
75. Kyôgoku Takatsugu
76. Natsuka Masaie

—Ise—
77. Fukushima Masanori
78. Ujiie Yukihiro
79. Takigawa Taketoshi
80. Wakebe Mitsuyoshi
81. Fukuda Nobutaka
82. *Yamazaki Masakatsu*
83. Tsutsui Sadatsugu
84. Okamoto Munenori
85. *Inaba Michiyuki*
86. Furuta Shigekatsu
87. Seki Kazumasa ****

—Shima—
88. Kuki Moritaka
89. *Horiuchi Ujiyoshi*
90. Sugiwaka Ujimune
91. Kuwayama Kazuharu

—Yamato—
92. Mashita Nagamori

—Izumi—
93. Kode Hideharu

—Settsu—
94. Katakiri Kasumoto ††††
95. Yamazaki Iemori

—Kinnai area—
96. Arima Noriyori,
Oda Yûraku,
Tsuda Nobunari,
Ishikawa Sadamichi,
Taga Hidekazu,
Yokohama Shigekatsu, etc.

—Tango—
97. Hosokawa Tadaoki

—Tanba—
98. Bessho Yoshinori
99. Onoki Shigekatsu,
Oda Nobutsutsu, etc.
100. Maeda Shigekatsu
101. *Kasuya Takenori*
102. Kinoshita Iesada ††††

—Awaji—
103. Wakizaka Yasuharu ****

—Inaba—
104. Itsukimura Masahiro ****
105. Miyabe Yoshimasa
106. Sugihara Nagafusa

107. Kakimuro Akinari
108. Miyabe Nagafusa
109. Kamei Korenori
110. Kinoshita Shigekata

—Hôki—
111. Nanjô Tadanari

—Izumo—
112. Kikkawa Hiroie ****

—Misaka, Bitchû, Bizen—
113. *Ukita Hideie*

—Bitchû, Bingo, Iwami,
Suô, Aki, Nagato—
114. *Môri Terumoto*

—Sanuki—
115. Ikoma Chikumasa

—Awa—
116. Hachisuka Iemasa

—Tosa—
117. *Chôsokabe Morichika*

—Igo—
118. Katô Yoshiaki
119. Ogawa Suketada ****
120. *Ikeda Hiroie*
121. *Ankokuji Ekei*
122. Tôdô Takatora

—Chikuzen—
123. Kobayakawa Hideaki ****

—Buzen—
124. Môri Katsunobu
125. Kuroda Nagamasa

—Bungo—
126. Takenaka Shigetoshi *
127. *Kakimi Kazunao*
128. *Kumadani Naomori*
129. Fukuhara Naotaka
130. Nakagawa Hidenari **
131. *Ôta Kazuyoshi*
132. *Môri Takamasa*

—Hyûga—
133. Takahashi Motokane *
134. Akizuki Kanenaga ***
135. Itô Suketaka

—Satsuma, Ôsumi, Hyûga
136. *Shimazu Yoshihisa*

—Higo—
137. Sagara Yorifusa ****
138. Konishi Yukinaga
139. Katô Kiyomasa

—Chikugo—
140. *Tachibana Muneshige*
141. *Môri Hidetsutsu*

—Hizen—
142. Nabeshima Naoshige
143. Terazawa Hirotaka
144. Ômura Yoshiaki ††††
145. Matsumura Shigenobu
146. Arima Harunobu ††††

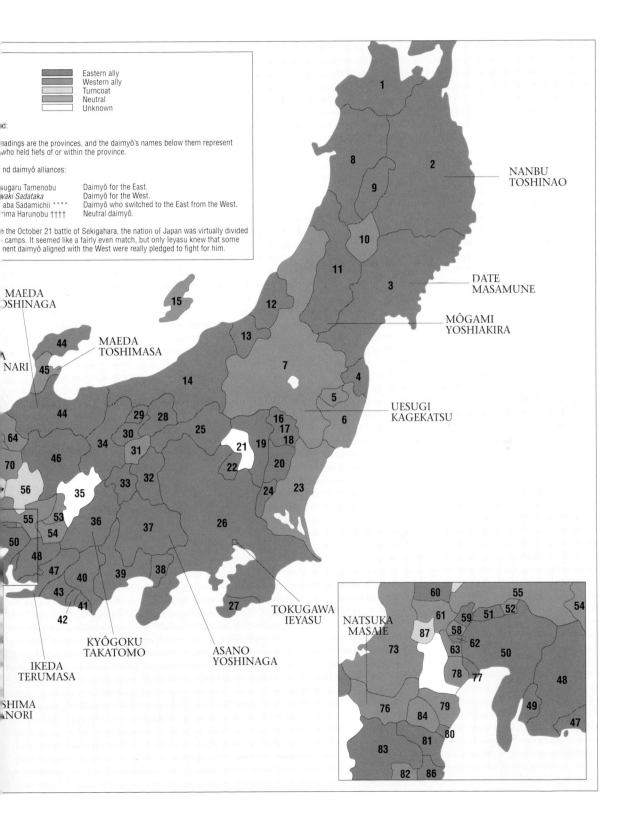

...d:

...adings are the provinces, and the daimyô's names below them represent
...who held fiefs of or within the province.

...nd daimyô alliances:

...ugaru Tamenobu   Daimyô for the East.
...waki *Sadataka*   Daimyô for the West.
...aba Sadamichii ****   Daimyô who switched to the East from the West.
...rima Harunobu ††††   Neutral daimyô.

...e the October 21 battle of Sekigahara, the nation of Japan was virtually divided
... camps. It seemed like a fairly even match, but only Ieyasu knew that some
...nent daimyô aligned with the West were really pledged to fight for him.

NANBU
TOSHINAO

DATE
MASAMUNE

MÔGAMI
YOSHIAKIRA

MAEDA
OSHINAGA

MAEDA
TOSHIMASA

NARI

UESUGI
KAGEKATSU

TOKUGAWA
IEYASU

NATSUKA
MASAIE

KYÔGOKU
TAKATOMO

ASANO
YOSHINAGA

IKEDA
TERUMASA

SHIMA
NORI

even on his own side – to be no great warrior or general. Kiyomasa had more than once referred to him as a civilian butting into military affairs. He had fought, and he could command troops, but ultimately his gifts were not those of a strategist or tactician; even Hideyoshi had appointed him inspector general, giving him a staff position rather than a direct command of his own.

Môri Terumoto (1553–1625), seven years Mitsunari's senior, was the nominal commander-in-chief of the Western Army. The Môri clan was ancient and powerful, and they had far more men and matériel at their disposal than had Mitsunari. With Maeda Toshiie dead and his legacy spread among his heirs, Terumoto had become one of the most wealthy daimyô alive. The respective financial power of Ieyasu and Terumoto can be clearly understood through a popular saying that Ieyasu could make a road of rice from the Kantô plain to Kyôto, and Terumoto could make a bridge of silver and gold from his domains to the capital.

Terumoto was worried about the potential loss of his provinces or even his life should he make the wrong choice and back the loser. His personal holdings were calculated at 1.2 million koku yearly, so this was no small concern. As he saw it, the victory in the coming struggle could go either way. He was leaning toward Ieyasu's position until Ankokuji Ekei, one of Terumoto's chief counsellors and a strong proponent of Hideyori's cause, convinced him to back Mitsunari. Ekei had also convinced Kikkawa Hiroie, Terumoto's cousin (and therefore another Môri Clan daimyô) to side with Mitsunari.

Mitsunari had been responsible for forming the anti-Tokugawa alliance, but the Môri name and reputation was greater than his, and Terumoto was one of the five tairô officially responsible for the welfare of Hideyori and the late taikô's empire, so when Terumoto signed on, fellow daimyô Otani Yoshitsugu advised Mitsunari to step aside – at least publicly – and let Terumoto be made commander-in-chief. Mitsunari agreed to this, placing Ukita Hideie, another of the five tairô, as Terumoto's second-in-command.

Mitsunari's pay for stepping aside, however, was that he would continue to be the real commander, pulling all the strings, and that Terumoto would have to remain in Ôsaka Castle. This was the headquarters of the Toyotomi faction, as it had been the taikô's seat of power. This arrange-

Môri Terumoto (1553-1625) was the powerful and wealthy head of the mighty Môri clan. Though made nominal commander-in-chief by Mitsunari, Terumoto was forbidden to actually take part in the battle. As revenge for this slight, his clan's soldiers, one of the largest single contingents, would not move when ordered to attack. Afterwards, he would try to reconcile with Ieyasu, but the latter considered him a traitor unworthy of consideration. (From a contemporary portrait.)

ment while installing Terumoto as nominal head of the faction, guaranteed that he would have little or no influence over how the campaign would be waged or the battles fought.

Unfortunately for the Western Army, Terumoto was an excellent commander, and Mitsunari was only second-rate on a good day. The assignment didn't sit well with all members of the Môri clan. Kikkawa Hiroie was one of these, and it was he who convinced Terumoto that the best course of action was, in fact, no action at all.

Ukita Hideie (1572-1662) was the nominal second in command. He had been raised by Toyotomi Hideyoshi, and was understandably intensely loyal to the Toyotomi cause. During the Korean Campaign, the taikô had named him general-in-chief (gensui), and he performed admirably. He was one of the five regents (tairô) responsible for governing in Hideyori's name. He ruled the rich provinces of Bizen and Mimasaka, and most of Bitchû, making him quite wealthy. On 21 October he favoured a night assault on the Tokugawa forces, and advised Mitsunari that striking while the Tokugawa were still deploying their forces in the foul weather would be certain victory. Mitsunari demurred, however, preferring a clear target he could see. Hideie was 28 years old.

Konishi Yukinaga (1560–1600) was one of the most powerful Christian daimyô. He had shared command of the vanguard of the first Korean invasion (1592) with fiercely anti-Christian Katô Kiyomasa; as unlikely and potentially explosive a combination as any that could have been made. Yukinaga had performed admirably, even forcing the Korean royal family to flee the capital; yet for some reason he and Mitsunari seem to have been

lumped together as civilian administrators rather than military officers. His whole career seemed to involve sharing with Kiyomasa, even to the extent of their fief, for each man had half of the province of Higa on Kyûshu. The dislike was deep and mutual. Along with Shimazu Yoshihiro, he would bring up the rearguard. He was 39 years old in 1600.

THE TURNCOATS

Several major daimyô in the Western Army switched sides or failed to attack during the battle, assuring a Tokugawa victory. It is safe to say that the pivotal rôle in these defections was played by Kobayakawa Hideaki (1582-1602). Had he not betrayed Mitsunari, the Eastern Army may well have been destroyed entirely.

Ôsaka Castle was the seat of Toyotomi authority. Here resided Hideyori, the late taikô's heir, and it was here too that Môri Terumoto was placed as 'commander' of the Western Army. This modern reconstruction follows the pattern of the Toyotomi structure.

everal clans on the loyalist side
efected outright or effected neu-
rality at the last moment by
olding their positions and fail-
g to engage the Eastern army
hen ordered to do so. The crests
f some of them are depicted
ere. From left to right:
obayakawa, Kikkawa,
Vakizaka, Ogawa.

Hideaki was a young man at Sekigahara, just 19 years old. It is fascinating to reflect that with all the cumulative years of experience spread out
among the commanders of both sides, the tide of battle was decided by the
emotional ties of one young man.

Hideaki was, in fact, the nephew of Hideyoshi's wife Ne-Ne, and had
also been adopted as a foster son by the taikô. He had grown up in the
care of Kuroda Yoshitaka. (Yoshitaka, baptised a Christian and named
Simeon, was the father of another famous Christian general, Kuroda
Nagamasa.) In addition to being both the nephew and foster son of
Hideyoshi, he was a grandson of the great Môri Motonari, and therefore
yet another cousin of Môri Terumoto. The convoluted interpersonal relationships of these great lords was the result of giving children in marriage
to seal alliances; only occasionally did it actually result in the desired effect
of assuring peace.

Hideaki's relationships with Ieyasu and Mitsunari went back to the
deceased taikô's attempt to conquer Korea. On the basis of his ties with
Hideyoshi, the 15-year-old Hideaki had been made commander of the army
in 1597, with Kuroda Yoshitaka as his advisor. When the generals under
Hideaki quarrelled and thereby brought about the failure of the campaign,
one of their number, Ishida Mitsunari, had denounced Hideaki as an
incompetent, and the taikô had ordered the latter to resign and return
home in disgrace. In Japan, Ieyasu had intervened on Hideaki's behalf, and
reconciled Hideyoshi and his foster son.

It is safe to say that Hideaki never forgot the slight by Mitsunari, and
never forgot the favour he owed to Ieyasu. In fact, Hideaki was on his way
to join Ieyasu when the war council was called in Ôsaka, and Mitsunari
himself talked Hideaki into joining the loyalist cause.

Mitsunari promised to make the young general the new kanpaku in
return for joining the loyalist cause, and place Hideyori, his foster brother, in his care. (One can only assume that Hideyori would then take the
title taikô.) It was a great offer, and one by which the young lord must
have been sorely tempted. For his part, Ieyasu promised to reward Hideaki
with two substantial domains for his allegiance.

Hideaki even went to his adoptive mother, Hideyoshi's widow, to ask
her what to do. Surprisingly, she told him to follow his conscience – and
then suggested that his conscience should lead him to Ieyasu.

The question Hideaki faced as he began to march, under the banners of
the Western Army, was which of the two men he trusted more – or less.
As a child he had been very bright, and everyone had remarked on his
mental acuity. Now he was faced with the most difficult – and dangerous
– decision of his life.

OPPOSING ARMIES

The Eastern and Western armies were virtually identical in make-up. Those commanders too young to have been veterans of the civil war of the last half of the 16th century were veterans of Hideyoshi's Korean conflict. Both armies were well-trained, well-equipped and well-disciplined.

STRUCTURE AND ORGANISATION

There was little in the way of 'rank' as we understand it in modern military usage. Those daimyô who commanded their own clansmen are usually referred to in English as generals; so a general might command anything from 500 troops to several thousand. Beneath the daimyô were direct vassals and trusted family retainers as officers. In the case of the Tokugawa, several great generals under Ieyasu's command were also heads of their

Officers commanded and led from horseback. This statue of one of the Toda lords of Ogaki Castle, in the castle grounds, is typical of the mounted warrior of the end of the 16th century. Toda Kazuaki (1542-1604) fought for Ieyasu, and in 1634 his son was invested as lord of what had been Ishida Mitsunari's personal castle. It was a mark of great favour.

EASTERN ARMY: SEKIGAHARA, 21 October 1600

Tokugawa Ieyasu	30,000	Katô Yoshiaki	3000
Honda Tadakatsu	500	Kuroda Nagamasa	5400
Hosokawa Tadaoki	5000	Kyôgoku Takatomo	3000
Ii Naomasa	3600	Oda Yûraku	450
Matsudaira Tadayoshi	3000	Tanaka Yoshimasa	3000
Tsutsui Sadatsugu	2850	Terazawa Hirotaka	2400
Arima Toyouji	900	Tôdô Takatora	2490
Asano Yukinaga	6510	Yamanouichi Kazutoyo	2058
Fukushima Masanori	6000	Yoshida Shigekatsu	1200
Ikeda Terumasa	4560		
Ikoma Kazumasa	1830		
Kanamori Nagachika	1140	**Total**	**88,888**

Due to the feudal make-up of the armies, nothing corresponding to a conventional corps, brigade or regiment existed. Greater lords had lesser lords under them, and so on. Well over 100,000 men who were not at Sekigahara itself were also 'involved' in the campaigns in Mino and neighboring provinces. They were held up in castle seiges or maintaining strongholds elsewhere. The following orders of battle represents the major commanders of both sides who were at the battle itself on 21 October, 1600. The numbers are not entirely certain, but they are agreed upon by most authorities. Modern scholars put the total number of men in the field that day at between 170,000 and 200,000.

WESTERN ARMY: SEKIGAHARA, 21 OCTOBER 1600

MÔRI TERUMOTO*	—	Shimazu Yoshihiro	1500
Ishida Mitsunari	4000	Shimazu Toyohisa	(750)
Shima Sakon	(1000)	Toda Shigemasa	
Gamo Bitchû	(1000)	& Hiratsuka Tamehiro	1500
Akaza Naoyasu†	600	Toyotomi retainers	2000
Chôsokabe Morichika	6600	Ukita Hideie ††	17,000
Kikkawa Hiroie†	3000	Wakizaka Yasuharo ††	990
Môri Hidemoto	15,000		
Ankokuji Ekei	1800	**Total**	**81,890**
Kobayakawa Hideaki†	15,600		
Konishi Yukinaga	4000		
Kuchiki Mototsuna†	600		
Natsuka Masaie	1500		
Ogawa Suketada†	2100		
Ôtani Yoshitsugu	600		
Ôtani Yoshikatsu			
& Kinoshita Yorichika	3500		

* Not present, in nominal command, but based in Ôsaka Castle.

† Traitors to the Western cause.

†† Nominally second-in-command.

Notes: numbers in parentheses indicate the size of a sub-command taken from the commander's unit, the full force of which appears above.

own clans (the Honda, Hosokawa, Ii and others), which made them generals under a general — a familiar Western concept. Still, one could refer to Hosokawa, for example, as 'one of Ieyasu's captains'.

This mix of rank and position, and the varying size of troop contingents make it difficult to create an order of battle as it is commonly understood. The usual modern distinctions of corps, division, brigade, regiment, and so on, are completely out of place. Each clan or functioning body may be considered a division, and the larger sub-units may be considered brigades, but there is no direct correlation.

The relationship between vassals or allies and their single overall commander was similar to the combined allied armies of the Second World War; there were both internal chains of command and overall external unifying chains of command.

These three warriors represent the Ashigaru, the lions share of both armies. Their armour and weapons were inexpensive and simple. The man on the left wears a simple belly-plate, the one in the middle a one-size-fits-all variation of the standard okegawa dô, and the man on the right a folding armour of hexagonal plates.

On many occasions this nebulous organisation, combined with the egos of the generals, nearly led to disaster; occasionally it did so, when the generals refused to follow the orders of a commanding general. For example, during the Sekigahara campaign, the Eastern Army (the Tokugawa faction) was attacking the Western stronghold of Gifu Castle. Two of the attacking generals, Ikeda Terumasa and Fukushima Masanori, argued over who would attack the castle first, and finally challenged each other to a duel over the issue. Fortunately cooler heads suggested that one should attack the front and the other attack the rear.

This highlights a problem the Japanese armies had during this period. No matter how well laid, plans were at the disposal of those with more interest in personal reputation and honour than overall outcome. It is easy to say that they were just being short-sighted, but incidents like this occurred in Korea as well. In fact, one can legitimately wonder what they might have accomplished on the continent if there had been less ill-will and more co-operation among the various commanders. Perhaps it is because Ieyasu, a far-sighted strategist, saw this as a problem that he moved as slowly as he did; he wanted to be sure that his orders would be followed and things go according to plan.

Under the commanders, discipline was severe and swift. Everyone had a rôle and knew what is was; everyone had a place and knew it. Failure could mean being stripped of rank, banished or even killed.

ARMS AND ARMOUR

Some daimyô provided uniform armours for their troops, to boost morale and aid recognition –as with Ii Naomasa's famous 'Red Devils'. Another daimyô famous for his uniform was Date Masamune, who equipped his entire army – from the lowest troops to the commanders – with four-sided solid armours called yukinoshita dô, with only the fittings and details marking any difference in rank.

Other daimyô handed out whatever they had available; others provided a stipend to allow their troops to buy gear they wanted. Many troops supplemented their armour allowance with the time-honoured tradition of looting the dead, acquiring a better helmet, weapon, or suit of armour from the fallen enemy. Although often officially discouraged, it was far from uncommon.

The ashigaru, the low-ranked men that made up the bulk of the army, usually got the least expensive equipment. Their body armour was often a suit of small plates held together by mail and designed to fold away into a

The average warrior in the field probably wore a simple but complete armour such as this. The solidly riveted cuirass, called an okegawa dô, could even be made shot-proof. (Yoroi no Kôzan-dô)

small package, called tatami gusoku (folding armour); a simple cuirass of solidly riveted steel lames, called an okegawa dô; or a hara-ate (armour that protected the front but not the back).

Armour for the average soldier consisted of a dô (cuirass), and some form of kabuto (helmet). In addition, they had kote, which were padded sleeves with integral splints of lacquered metal and mail sewn on. Most had some kind of leg armour, even if it was only splinted shin defences called suneate. A split-apron like piece of armour (called haidate), designed to protect the thighs, was often worn; the latter were uncomfortable on the march, but those who were issued them usually took advantage of the protection they offered, even if only on the field.

The variety of armour and different methods of decorating it at the close of the 16th century was incredible. Even something as simple as a cuirass of horizontal lames solidly riveted one to the other might have flush rivets, domed rivets or even large decorative fasteners; it could also have one of a dozen different 'lines' of cut (straight lines, saw-toothed edges, deep rolling curves, arrow-head shaped cut-outs and so on).

One of the most striking features of Japanese armour of the period was the sashimono, a long banner worn from a crossbar and pole arrangement attached to the back of the armour. These banners were marked with the mon, or crest, of the commander of the samurai's unit. Naturally, Lords didn't usually wear sashimono; they had standards and standard-bearers. The banners of different units within an army could be similar, to provide instant recognition. (In Akira Kurosawa's films Ran and Kagemusha, these banners are in evidence in all battle scenes; in reality there would have been thousands.)

Their primary weapons were long lances called yari, which were even used by cavalry. In English they are often called spears, but this gives the mistaken impression that they were missile weapons; in fact they were

RIGHT *A page sits on the floor next to a stand for matchlocks. In castles, some lords had their guns on display in the same manner as their swords. Note the variety in ornamentation and size. The page wears an outfit called a kamishimo, which was the standard day-to-day wear of most samurai at this period. (Kiyosu castle)*

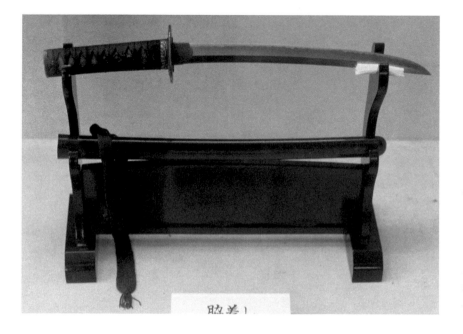

LEFT *The wakizashi was the companion sword to the longer, deadly katana or tachi. The blade was anywhere from a foot to two feet in length. Contrary to popular modern opinion, it was not reserved for committing suicide. (Gifu Castle)*

28

Tokugawa Ieyasu is supposed to have worn a European armour at the battle. Several suits of Spanish or Portuguese make had been given by foreign potentates as gifts to curry the favor of powerful lords. Invariably they were altered to suit Japanese taste. To his right stands Honda Tadatsugu one of Ieyasu's most loyal retainers and one of the Eastern Army's commanders at Sekigahara. To his left stands 'The One-Eyed Dragon', Date Masamune, another loyal Tokugawa vassal. At the time of Sekigahara Masamune was engaged in a campaign against Uesugi Kagekatsu and his vassals in northern Honshu.

Kuroda Nagamasa here wears a jinbaori, or camp coat, over his armour. Generals wore them in camp, seldom in the field. Considering the chaos at Sekigahara, some generals possibly wore theirs all day, in and out of camp. Accompanying him is Ii Naomasa whose 'Red Devils' launched the charge which opened the battle. The banner of the samurai with them shows him to be of the Tokugawa clan.

never thrown. Most yari were around nine feet long, although many clans were uniformly equipped with longer or shorter ones.

The secondary weapons were swords, which they carried in pairs: a long sword called a tachi or katana, and a smaller sword called a wakizashi. Some carried dirks as well. The poorest soldiers carried at least the longer sword, with a dirk or two in reserve.

The dirk was generally used to remove the heads of the slain enemy as a battle trophy. At the end of the day, heads would be counted, and those of important people (daimyô and generals, say) would be presented to the commander for a head-viewing ceremony.

Virtually every clan in both the Eastern and Western armies had units of dozens or even hundreds of arquebusiers called teppô tai. The weapon had been introduced from Portugal, by accident, in 1542 and by 1600 was being made domestically in huge quantities. It had changed the face of Japanese warfare. No longer was posturing, making speeches, and single combat the overriding method of warfare; now the lowliest footsoldier could instantly slay the mightiest lord from a great distance.

The arquebusier units had largely supplanted the units of archers common in battles only a few decades before. Bows were still in use, but their importance was greatly diminished. When the loyalist Shimazu clan arrived at Sekigahara with their archers, and with old Shimazu Yoshihiro himself carrying a bow, the rest of the army viewed it as rather quaint.

OPPOSING PLANS

Uesugi Kagekatsu (1555-1623), the quarrelsome lord of Aizu, had planned to strike Ieyasu from one direction while Mitsunari struck from the other. Instead, Date Masamune and Môgami Yoshiakira kept him busy. In the end, he submitted to Ieyasu, and even took part in the 1615 siege of Ôsaka Castle under Tokugawa orders. From a contemporary portrait.

Ieyasu's actions following the death of Toyotomi Hideyoshi had caused concern among the councils of the bugyô and tairô. Most acrimonious of all was Ishida Mitsunari. Even before getting the bugyô and tairô to submit the letter of complaints against Ieyasu, on 22 August 1600, Mitsunari had begun consolidating his forces in earnest.

Mitsunari had made a secret compact with daimyô Uesugi Kagekatsu of Aizu (located north and east of Ieyasu's home base in the Kantô) that both would raise armies and attack Ieyasu. The latter, caught on either side, would be crushed between them. Ieyasu seems to have had intelligence of Mitsunari's intentions, and the plan failed. Ieyasu had warned his allies in the east to be ready to respond to hostile moves on the part of Kagekatsu, so when Kagekatsu moved, Ieyasu was ready, though he allowed Mitsunari and Kagekatsu to believe he had swallowed the bait.

With the benefit of foresight – or effective use of spies – Ieyasu was able to move very slowly towards the east to deal with Kagekatsu, and then rapidly back westwards to engage Mitsunari, whom he considered the real threat.

Mitsunari had been plotting against Ieyasu for a long time, and through flattery or promises of reward had been able to win over many who'd originally been counted in the Eastern camp. However, Mitsunari's personality defects often undermined the loyalty of these converts. He was noted for a certain heavy-handedness, and a temper that had backfired on more than one occasion.

One of Mitsunari's greatest mistakes was in his handling of the hostage situation as the stormclouds gathered. The taking of hostages was common, so Mitsunari resolved to place in hazard the wives and families of Tokugawa loyalists who had been left in Osaka after Ieyasu had vacated that castle for Edo in July. One of these women was a baptised Christian, Gracia, the wife of Tokugawa retainer and general Hosokawa Tadaoki. A student of Latin and Portuguese, Donna Gracia was a very educated and refined lady. She was determined that she would not be an impediment to her husband's actions and thus an impediment to their lord, Ieyasu. When Mitsunari sent men to place her under arrest, rather than submit she ordered a servant to kill her and to set fire to their mansion. This action so stunned all of Ôsaka that Mitsunari was only able to place token guard forces at the homes of the hostage-wives of Tokugawa generals, most of whom then escaped in the night, including the wives of Katô Kiyomasa, Kuroda Nagamasa and Ikeda Terumasa.

This blunder served to convince many who were wavering that Mitsunari was not the kind of man they wanted to support. It was one thing to take a hostage; it was another for an intended hostage to commit suicide and immolate herself to thwart it, and for it to have been allowed to happen.

If some of this is beginning to sound familiar as part of the plot of the novel Shôgun, there is a reason for that. If one substitutes Hosokawa Gracia for Mariko, Tokugawa Ieyasu for Toranaga, Ishida Mitsunari for Ishido and even William Adams for Blackthorne, the novel reveals a historical basis. Except for the romance between William Adams and Hosokawa Gracia (who may never have even met) the book gives an excellent overview of the machinations before Sekigahara, and virtually everyone in the novel has a historical counterpart.

When Ieyasu began to move back west, it was his intention to gain control of the Nakasendô and Tôkaidô roads, mask Mitsunari in Ôgaki, and take out the latter's base of operations in Sawayama. Then, he suspected, the coalition would fall apart of itself.

THE SEKIGAHARA CAMPAIGN

The one-day battle of Sekigahara was not an isolated conflict; it was part of a true campaign. The struggle that culminated in the narrow valley around the village of Sekigahara on 21 October 1600 had actually begun in earnest in July of that year.

Uesugi Kagekatsu was involved in building up his domain's defences when Ieyasu sent word to Aizu from Ôsaka in May asking him to explain his actions. The reply came not directly from Kagekatsu but from his chief counsellor, a man named Naoe Kanetsugu, who responded with sarcasm, saying that while citified samurai spent their time collecting tea implements, country samurai collected weapons.

Echigo, the neighbouring province to Aizu, had as its lord Hori Hideharu. He too was alarmed at the actions of Kagekatsu. The belligerent lord of Aizu had 80,000 men working round the clock building a new castle and several defensive points around it. He was also building roads that could be used to move large numbers of troops.

Kagekatsu went so far as to make an attempt on the life of one of Ieyasu's messengers, a man Kagekatsu's advisors (perhaps accurately) took for a spy. Ieyasu, incensed at this affront to his authority, sent for Kagekatsu, ordering him to come personally to Ôsaka to explain his actions. When no satisfactory reply was forthcoming, Ieyasu decided that his only option was to call for the coalition to put the Uesugi down, so on 12 July he held a war council in Ôsaka to plan a campaign against Aizu with his generals. On 22 July his chief allies in the outlying regions left Osaka for their home provinces to prepare for war. If not against the Uesugi specifically, Ieyasu knew that he would need to have people in every part of the country to keep things under control when hostilities broke out with Mitsunari.

Ieyasu gathered his army, and on 24 July, to Mitsunari's secret glee, began a leisurely march eastwards from Ôsaka Castle.

For his part, Kagekatsu was not concerned, as he was certain that before he was in any real danger Mitsunari would be sweeping up behind Ieyasu. When Kagekatsu struck, a few weeks later, Tokugawa allies Môgami Yoshiakira and Date Masamune immediately counter-attacked. Maeda Toshinaga would have joined as well, but he was suddenly preoccupied with a war against his brother and others who supported the loyalists. A

The yarô-kabuto ('bumpkin helmet') was designed to represent the head of a peasant, with closely cropped hair. It was another of the uncommon helmet forms that appeared during the latter years of the 16th century. Like most, it was built up on the base of a three-plate zûnari. (Yoroi no Kôzan-dô)

fourth daimyô, Satake Yoshinobu, refused to take arms against Kagekatsu, but with the forces of the Môri and Date, the situation was under control.

Ieyasu stopped for the night in Fushimi Castle on 25 July, spending the evening talking and drinking with the castle garrison commander, an old and trusted friend named Torii Mototada. Both knew that once hostilities began in earnest, Fushimi would be one of Mitsunari's first targets, and that there was no way Mototada would be able to hold it. The castle would fall and he would die, and both he and Ieyasu knew it. Their parting the next morning became a popular subject for artists for generations, so emotional was it for both of them.

Ishida Mitsunari called a war council even as Ieyasu was marching eastwards from Osaka. On 17 August the chief conspirators met in Mitsunari's castle of Sawayama. Ukita Hideie was Mitsunari's deputy, and among those in attendance were old Shimazu Yoshihiro (then 65 year old – practically ancient for a daimyô), lord of Satsuma; Kobayakawa Hideaki; Nabeshima Katsushige, son of Nabeshima Naoshige, lord of Saga; Chôsokabe Morichika, lord of Tosa; and Ôtani Yoshitsugu, lord of Tsuruga. The latter had in fact been on his way to join Ieyasu in his campaign against Uesugi Kagekatsu, but Mitsunari had intercepted him and convinced him to join with the loyalists instead. It was a decision Yoshitsugu would regret for the rest of his life.

Ieyasu advanced slowly, which enabled him to monitor Mitsunari's machinations. He had full confidence in Masamune and Yoshiakira's ability to contain Kagekatsu. For his part, Mitsunari was certain that Ieyasu would engage the Uesugi before long, and then Mitsunari could move his army up the Nakasendô and Tôkaidô (the two trunk roads between Edo and the capital) and fall upon him from the rear.

Ieyasu reached Edo on 10 August, and remained there until 1 September, when he moved north to Ôyama with his 50,000-strong army. In the meantime, Date Masamune, Maeda Toshinaga and the others were keeping Uesugi Kagekatsu busy; Ieyasu was prepared to strike at Kagekatsu, but did not expect to have to do so.

In Ôsaka, Kikkawa Hiroie was angry over the Môri slight by Mitsunari which forced their clan leader, Terumoto, now nominally the commander of their forces, to remain out of the action. He responded by secretly sending messages to Ieyasu's generals Kuroda Nagamasa and Ii Naomasa promising that when it was time to fight, the 36,000-man Môri division would not engage the Eastern Army. Môri Hidemoto, Terumoto's cousin and the man who was to lead the Môri in Terumoto's stead, urged Terumoto to submit to the Tokugawa before hostilities could break out. He knew the dangers of losing.

On 27 August loyalist forces set upon Fushimi Castle just as Ieyasu and Torii Mototada had expected. The garrison defended it well, holding off for ten days, for Mototada knew that their duty was to delay the Western Army in any way they could; capitulation wasn't an option.

The defence was getting tired, but could have held longer had not a castle tower been set afire by a traitor within, whose wife and children had been threatened with crucifixion by Mitsunari. There was little left to do. With the castle beginning to burn and the garrison reduced to just 200 men, Mototada led several vicious sorties from the castle against the attackers. Only when it was clear that there was nothing left to hold off the enemy with, and the defenders had been reduced to ten, did the remaining Tokugawa samurai commit suicide as the castle burned around them. It was 6 September. Mitsunari had won, but it had cost him nearly 3000 of his own men to take Fushimi.

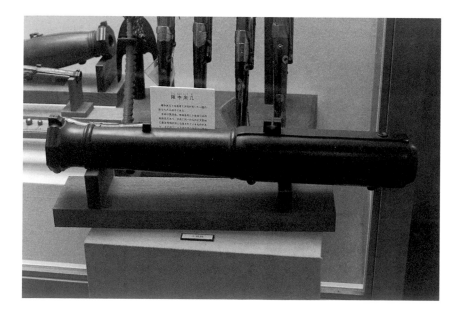

A larger cannon such as this would have been used during the sieges of Ueda, Ôtsu, and Fushimi castles. This one was designed specifically to shoot 'fire arrows' – exploding, incendiary missiles. Some cannon were actually breach-loading. Several surviving cannon were cast in the form of a dragon, with the muzzle as the dragon's mouth. (Nagakute Battlefield Museum)

IEYASU'S MOVEMENTS, JULY-OCTOBER 1600

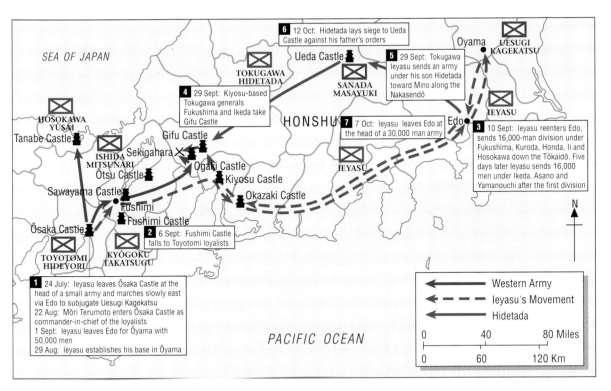

6 12 Oct: Hidetada lays siege to Ueda Castle against his father's orders

5 29 Sept: Tokugawa Ieyasu sends an army under his son Hidetada toward Mino along the Nakasendô

4 29 Sept: Kiyosu-based Tokugawa generals Fukushima and Ikeda take Gifu Castle

7 7 Oct: Ieyasu leaves Edo at the head of a 30,000 man army

3 10 Sept: Ieyasu reenters Edo, sends 16,000-man division under Fukushima, Kuroda, Honda, Ii and Hosokawa down the Tôkaidô. Five days later Ieyasu sends 16,000 men under Ikeda, Asano and Yamanouchi after the first division

2 6 Sept: Fushimi Castle falls to Toyotomi loyalists

1 24 July: Ieyasu leaves Ôsaka Castle at the head of a small army and marches slowly east via Edo to subjugate Uesugi Kagekatsu
22 Aug: Môri Terumoto enters Ôsaka Castle as commander-in-chief of the loyalists
1 Sept: Ieyasu leaves Edo for Ôyama with 50,000 men
29 Aug: Ieyasu establishes his base in Ôyama

SEA OF JAPAN

HONSHU

PACIFIC OCEAN

Western Army
Ieyasu's Movement
Hidetada

| 0 | 40 | 80 Miles |
| 0 | 60 | 120 Km |

With Fushimi fallen, the Western allies could meet up safely with Mitsunari in Ôgaki Castle for the march north and east, where they would attack Ieyasu from the rear, taking him in his home province of Mikawa.

By 10 September Ieyasu was back in Edo, preparing his forces for the final confrontation.

On 15 September Mitsunari entered Ogaki with images of Ieyasu's imminent fall playing in his head. He had no idea that Ieyasu was already planning a return to Osaka.

Kiyosu and Gifu castles, only some 15 miles from Ôgaki, were also very close to the Tôkaidô and Nakasendô roads, which were only about 20 miles apart at that point. Whoever controlled those two castles controlled the traffic. As it was, the castles were held by partisans from opposing camps, and each camp was determined to hold theirs and obtain mastery over the other. Ôsaki Genba (called Oni Genba, or 'Devil Genba' by his enemies), held Kiyosu Castle for Fukushima Masanori, allied with Ieyasu. Oda Nobunaga's grandson (who had been raised by the taikô) was in command of the strategically-sited Gifu Castle. He had been advised by his counsellors to side with Ieyasu, but he had elected instead to favour the loyalist cause.

Aware of the dangers the 19-year-old Oda Hidenobu posed as Nobunaga's grandson, Ieyasu despatched 16,000 men along the Tôkaidô under Fukushima Masanori, Kuroda Nagamasa, Honda Tadakatsu, Ii Naomasa and Hosokawa Tadaoki, to first secure Kiyosu and then take Gifu

SPREY MILITARY JOURNAL

TERNATIONAL REVIEW OF MILITARY HISTORY

King Richard III: Villain or Victim?

Mosby snatches a Yankee General

US Marines on the Western Front 1918

views
s, Games
del Kits

Fascinating articles on military history from antiquity to modern times

The Wars of the Roses
Terence Wise
Illustrated by Gerry Embleton

CAMPAIGN 69
NAGASHINO 1575
SLAUGHTER AT THE BARRICADES
STEPHEN TURNBULL

OSPREY AIRCRAFT OF THE ACES · 32
French Aces of World War 2
Barry Ketley

WARRIOR SERIES 16
BRITISH TOMMY 1914–18
WEAPONS · ARMOUR · TACTICS
MARTIN PEGLER · MIKE CHAPPELL

ARMIES OF THE PHARAOHS
MARK HEALY · ILLUSTRATED BY ANGUS McBRIDE

NEW VANGUARD 33
M3 & M5 STUART LIGHT TANK 1940–1945
STEVEN J. ZALOGA · JIM LAURIER

THE SAMURAI
ANTHONY J BRYANT ILLUSTRATED BY ANGUS McBRIDE

MEN-AT-ARMS 339
THE KING'S GERMAN LEGION (2) 1812–1816
MIKE CHAPPELL

TEXAS RANGERS
TEXAS RANGER
DR STEPHEN HARDIN
ILLUSTRATED BY RICHARD HOOK

RENOWNED FOR OVER 30 YEARS
Visit Osprey at www.ospreypublishing.com

OSPREY MILITARY JOURNAL - From the world's leading publisher of illustrated military history. Bi monthly (six issues per year) 64 pages per issue fully illustrated in Osprey's unique style with artwork, maps, charts and photos. Fascinating articles on military history from ancient times to the present day and expert guidance for enthusiasts.

at all costs. Then, perhaps being cautious, he sent after them a further 15,000 men, under Ikeda Terumasa, Asano Yoshinaga and Yamanouchi Kazutoyo.

Ieyasu then sent a third large force – this time 36,000 strong – under the command of his son, Hidetada. This force was to go down the Nakasendô, through central Honshu. All the armies would rendezvous somewhere in the province of Mino, where Ieyasu would join them to take direct command.

The combined Tôkaidô divisions, now numbering 31,000, entered Kiyosu Castle and from there attacked Gifu Castle on 28 September, taking it with little effort. Gifu Castle, perched high atop a lonely mountain, was flying Eastern flags the next day. Oda Hidenobu was sent to the mountaintop monasteries on Kôyasan under guard. He had to wait for Ieyasu to decide his fate after the battles were all over; he was no longer a player.

Ieyasu himself left Edo on 7 October at the head of his own 30,000-man army, making a forced march towards the west. Unlike his slow trek to Edo, which had taken 40 days with only a few thousand men, Ieyasu would move an entire army back nearly the same distance in two weeks.

RIGHT *Perched high on a lonely mountain in Gifu City is Gifu Castle, Ieyasu's base from which he launched the attack at Sekigahara. It had been the castle of Oda Hidenobu, who chose to support Mitsunari, but two large Eastern forces under Fukushima Masanori and Kuroda Nagamasa had taken it. The castle was not rebuilt, and remained vacant throughout the Tokugawa shogunate. The current donjon is a modern reconstruction.*

THE SIEGES

As may be suspected from the attacks on Gifu and Kiyosu, castles, commanding strategic points were important to both sides. Several of the sieges of the Sekigahara campaign were ill-conceived and poorly executed however, and only served to keep soldiers away from more important battles elsewhere.

THE SIEGE WITH EMPTY CANNON

The various loyalist commanders had been courting Hosokawa Yûsai, Tadaoki's father, for some time. Having his support would be a great boost to morale for either side, for though an old man, he was a scholar and poet of great renown throughout the empire. Yûsai, however, would have none of Mitsunari's manoeuvrings, and he was appalled by the incident that had resulted in the death of his daughter-in-law, Gracia. He immediately left for his castle of Tanabe in the Tango province, and with his 500-man garrison declared for Ieyasu. It was virtual suicide. In mid-August, while Ieyasu was still in Oyama, supposedly preparing to deal with Uesugi Kagekatsu, 15,000 men under Ishida's flag surrounded the lonely castle and began the assault.

What should have been a quick victory for the loyalists proved to be something else entirely, but it was all their own fault. So great was the respect of Yûsai's opponents for him – many of whom in fact had been his pupils – that more often than not they 'forgot' to put shells in their cannon as they bombarded the castle.

Yûsai the scholar had many valuable scrolls and books of poetry in his castle, some of them ancient and literally irreplaceable. He asked for and received permission to send them to the emperor so that they wouldn't be destroyed in the siege. An imperial envoy soon arrived, and the loyalists called for a ceasefire (for want of a better term) to allow him in to receive the books. The envoy begged Yûsai, in the emperor's name, to surrender rather than risk his own valuable life, in what must have been apparent as a suicide stand. Despite his great fame as a man of letters, Yûsai considered himself first and last a samurai, and his life was defined by service to his lord, Ieyasu, so he refused to surrender.

Sanada Masayuki (1544-1608), besieged in Ueda Castle, managed to keep Tokugawa Hidetada busy long enough to cause him to miss the battle altogether. He sent his two sons to fight on opposite sides of the conflict. After the battle, he was condemned to death, but his son Nobuyuki (a son-in-law of Tokugawa vassal-general Honda Tadakatsu), who'd fought for Ieyasu, pleaded his case and won him a reprieve. Instead, he was banished to the Kii province where he died in exile. From a contemporary portrait.

Cannon were in existence in Japan, and were used briefly at Sekigahara, but not to much effect. They were primarily reserved for use in siege duty, and only rarely were used against infantry. On the other hand, the design of some matchlocks leaves the impression that they were intended to be virtual hand cannons. A small cannon and large-bore handgun, displayed side by side, show this relationship. Typical sizes of shot are shown below. Shot in Japan was measured by weight, not diameter. (Nagakute Battlefield Museum)

Fearing for Yûsai's life, the emperor himself ordered him to surrender the garrison. Yûsai had no choice but to obey, and on 19 October he ordered his men to march out the gate. The Western Army allowed him to pass. He retired to Kyôto to devote himself to his craft, but by the time he had surrendered, Yûsai had done his bit; during the two months of the siege 15,000 Western warriors had been kept preoccupied and too far from Sekigahara to have been of any good.

UEDA CASTLE

Tokugawa Ieyasu's third son (and heir apparent) Hidetada marched west from Edo along the Nakasendô with 36,000 men. He was under orders to mask the loyalist stronghold of Ueda Castle and continue the march, joining up with his father and the Tôkaidô divisions somewhere in Mino around 20 October. He decided instead to take the castle. Hidetada diverted his entire force and made straight for the loyalist fortress on 12 October.

Ueda Castle was held by Sanada Masayuki, who was in the unenviable position of having a son commanding troops in each army. His youngest son, Yukimura, was the husband of the daughter of Ôtani Yoshitsugu, one of Mitsunari's chief commanders; his eldest son, Nobuyuki, was the son-in-law of Honda Tadakatsu, one of the chief Tokugawa vassal generals.

Masayuki himself was no great friend of Ieyasu, owing to an ancient slight, but he still told Nobuyuki to fight for the Tokugawa, as that was where his loyalty lay, and Yukimura he sent to fight with Mitsunari.

Masayuki, at 56, was a skilled garrison commander – and a better general than Hidetada, who was only 21 – and he held off the superior Eastern forces for four days. Fearing he had delayed too much already, Hidetada finally broke off the siege on 16 October, and returned to his original route – westbound on the Nakasendô.

By the time Hidetada arrived at Sekigahara, Ieyasu was mopping up the enemy and counting heads.

OTSU CASTLE

Kyôgoku Takatsugu held Otsu Castle for Ieyasu. Situated very strategically on the south-west shore of Lake Biwa, the castle was vital to both armies; Ieyasu needed to keep it, and Mitsunari needed to take it.

On 13 October a force of 15,000 under Môri Motoyasu, Tachibana Muneshige and Tsukushi Hirokado took up positions near the castle, with the naval forces of Mashita Nagamori blockading the lake approach. The castle was designed as a series of concentric rings, or wards, with inner wards separated from the outer wards by moats fed from the lake itself, which the castle backed. Four causeways connected the outer ward of the castle to the mainland. Barring a naval attack, Otsu was virtually impregnable.

Motoyasu, with his command of 11,500, laid siege to the main causeway, Miidera-guchi, while Hirokado's 2500 took the Kyômachi-guchi

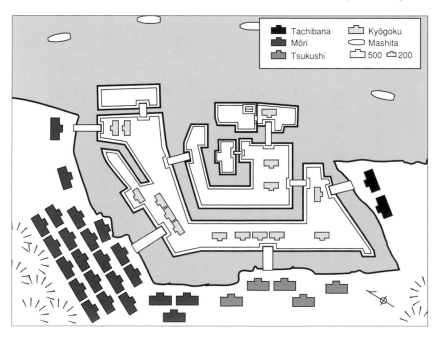

Tachibana | Kyôgoku
Môri | Mashita
Tsukushi | 500 | 200

The so-called three-plate helmet, perhaps the most common at the end of the 16th century, could be dressed up any number of ways. On this helmet of the Hineno school, a rare horse-hair plume is combined with a gilt crescent moon crest, enormous knobbed rivets, and highly ornate fukigaeshi ('blowbacks') bearing the owner's mon. (Yoroi no Kôzan-dô)

causeway and Muneshige's 1,000 set upon the Hamamachi-guchi causeway. The fourth was masked by units of Motoyasu's force, for as it abutted the lake, Motoyasu deemed it too difficult to overrun. The other bridges gave them plenty of room to work with.

The siege was a theatrical sideshow for the residents of Kyôto. Just as neighbouring townsmen did at the First Battle of Manassas in the American Civil War, Kyôto townsfolk – noble and peasant alike – took to their roofs and to the nearby mountainsides to have picnic lunches and watch warriors try to kill each other.

The defenders, 3000 in all, held out. Six days into the siege, Takatsugu sent a ninja, one of Japan's near-legendary spies and assassins, out on a daring (if unconventional) mission. The ninja stole into the Môri camp and made off with a few of their banners. Though it had been a dangerous operation, in essence it was a sarcastic jest. The next morning, the Môri samurai saw several of their banners flying from the walls of the inner compound.

The actual effect was slightly different than intended. When Tachibana Muneshige saw the banners, he thought Motoyasu had already achieved the castle, and that he, Muneshige, was terribly tardy in gaining his end. Between his haste to break the causeway's defence, and the Môri rage at the humiliating insult, the Western Army redoubled its efforts along all fronts. They even got a battery of cannon up on Mount Nagara to fire down into the castle grounds.

The assault was relentless, and the next day it succeeded. Even though the castle defences were reduced to rubble, there was no glory in the victory; the day after the Môri saw their banners flown over the castle walls was 21 October, the day of the great battle. Takatsugu had lost his command, but he kept 15,000 loyalists from the field.

CHOOSING THE FIELD

The arrival of Mitsunari's Western allies in Ogaki was slow, and Mitsunari was worried that Ieyasu would have the upper hand after all. It is interesting to note that even he was taken by surprise at the swiftness of the Tokugawa advance. Following his better instincts, he sent urgent messages to Môri Terumoto, who had returned to his own domain to raise his army, to urge him to make speed for Osaka with the bulk of the Môri forces – just in case. Unfortunately for Mitsunari, the messengers were taken by the enemy, and never reached Terumoto. A second message was sent, and the Môri – 30,000 strong – finally marched into Ôsaka.

Kobayakawa Hideaki had also sent out a messenger, only his was to Ieyasu. Hideaki promised to support the Tokugawa when the pitched battle finally took place.

Three days after receiving Hideaki's letter, on 17 October, Ieyasu reached Kiyosu. He had control of both of the castles commanding the two

A samurai of the teppo-tai in typical marching orders. Both Eastern and Western Army men spent days in this gear. This man wears a solidly-rivetted cuirass of steel lames, and carries a matchlock. The Honda clan of which this matchlockman is a retainer were Tokugawa vassals and fought for Ieyasu at Sekigahara.

roads, so could bypass Ogaki entirely and march his men right up either road and straight into Osaka or Sawayama (for the two roads merged into one just outside Kyôto). Ieyasu only had to leave a small contingent of troops by the Nakasendô, and Mitsunari would be masked in Ogaki, utterly unable to move.

Two days later, he was in Gifu Castle.

THE SKIRMISH IN AKASAKA

Ieyasu arrived in Akasaka, a small village facing the Western headquarters at Ôgaki Castle, around noon on 20 October. The main body of his Tôkaidô army had already been camped there for a few weeks. Ieyasu set up camp on a small hill called Okayama that commanded the vicinity. A narrow river, the Kuisegawa, ran by the hill, and a little way downstream on the opposite bank – less than three miles away – was Ogaki Castle. Just to the west was Mount Nangû, and beyond that, Sekigahara.

Ieyasu's arrival and proximity caused consternation in the loyalist castle. Some generals advised Mitsunari that a direct attack was imminent, while others felt Ieyasu knew he was still in no position to move against Ogaki.

Shima Sakon and a few other vassals talked Mitsunari into letting them test the enemy position by leading a small raiding party. Sakon took 500 men, and another vassal, Akashi Masataka, took 800, and they set out for Akasaka. Sakon split his force, taking half across the river and setting the rest up in ambush, while his compatriot sent his entire force across. The half of Sakon's force that crossed the bridge over the river conducted a brief raid to which Nakamura Kazuuji, one of Ieyasu's commanders, responded by sending several hundred men to counterstrike.

The Western forces withdrew back across the river, only to be pursued by the Eastern samurai. There Nakamura's men were attacked by the forces in ambush, and retreated back across the river, pursued this time by the Westerners, and now were set upon by the rest of the Western forces. Arima Toyouji sent several hundred men to support Nakamura's men. During the conflict the bridge was destroyed. The skirmish ended suddenly when dusk rendered further activity pointless.

The two forces limped back to their respective camps the worse for wear; little had been accomplished other than a break in an otherwise dull day. It did, however, mark the first time that both main bodies had made contact, although it was tentative contact and not supported by great force.

When the attack had begun, Ieyasu had just been sitting down to his lunch. His messengers had rushed in to tell him about the raid, but rather than call for his armour he simply scooped up his meal and went to the highest point in his command base – the roof – to watch the manoeuvrings of both armies. He was initially impressed by Nakamura's quick response, but when he saw his men chase the Westerners over the river, he commented that they had been taken in.

Mitsunari hadn't needed a skirmish to know he was in a tight spot. Ieyasu was in a position to command the Nakasendô, while he, Mitsunari, could be masked and bypassed with ease. He needed a point where he could

Ogaki Castle was the base from which Ishida launched his attack on Sekigahara. After Sekigahara, the castle would be rebuilt, and see an astonishing number of lords in a short time. Ieyasu's son held it briefly, as did the Ishikawa, Hisamatsu (cousins to Ieyasu), Okabe, Hisamatsu (again) and finally the Toda. The latter would hold the castle until the end of the Tokugawa shogunate in 1868. This modern reproduction replaces the original, which was destroyed by bombing in 1945.

intercept Ieyasu; Ôsaka and Sawayama were what mattered, not Ogaki.

It was at this point that old Shimazu Yoshihiro suggested a full-scale night-time assault on the Tokugawa position. He had observed them and their camp, noting that many seemed near exhaustion, and had been walking and eating and sleeping in their armour for two weeks. A night assault would have the advantage of surprise, as well. Ukita Hideie, the second-in-command, supported Yoshihiro's idea. It would be certain victory, he insisted.

Shima Sakon, Mitsunari's strategist, sneered at what he considered the cowardice implied in the idea. 'Night-time assaults are for weak forces against the strong,' he said. 'The numbers favour us. In a pitched battle, we will be the victors.' Hideie accepted the decision, but Yoshihiro was gravely insulted. Mitsunari would regret that insulting reply.

Mitsunari was faced with having to 'abandon' Ogaki to save Sawayama; there was no option. He compared his choice with risking the head to save an arm. But where to go?

Then he had a brilliant idea. One of the last of his Western allies to arrive had been Kobayakawa Hideaki, who had taken up position in a little village in a valley, right on the Nakasendô, where a spur from the Tôkaidô joins it, near another spur rounding Mount Ibuki going up to the third major road, the Hokkoku Kaidô (Northern Road), through Honshu. He'd have to run south around Mount Nangû to get there, but he could intercept Ieyasu's western push on the Nakasendô. Sekigahara was the perfect site.

That evening, about 7.00 pm on 20 October, while Ieyasu was settling down to relax, Mitsunari ordered a general withdrawal to the valley, some 12 miles behind Ogaki Castle. Leaving just 7500 men to garrison Ogaki, they set out south and west. The rain was just beginning to fall.

THE BATTLE

BEFORE DAWN

The rain fell in sheets, blown nearly horizontal by the wind. The night was cold and dark, and the Western troops advancing could scarcely make out their own banners. Once or twice divisions bumped into the rear guard of the divisions in front, provoking bursts of fear and excitement.

Mitsunari rode around the south pass behind Mount Nangû. His division reached Sekigahara around 1.00 am. Behind him was the rest of the Western Army. En route, he went to check on the positions of Ankokuji Ekei and Natsuka Masaie. Contented, Mitsunari rode on.

He headed to Mount Matsuo, where Kobayakawa Hideaki was bivouacked. Mitsunari congratulated Hideaki on his position, and indicated his intent to set up his command post on Mount Sasao, opposite. Mitsunari had heard unsettling rumours of a possible secret Môri pact with the Tokugawa, and wanted to take every precaution to prevent it. To protect his position, he extracted a promise from Hideaki that the Kobayakawa samurai would descend on the flank of the Eastern Army – whatever division presented itself most favourably for the attack – when they saw Mitsunari light a signal fire. Hideaki readily agreed, and Mitsunari, greatly relieved, set off again, this time for the pre-arranged position of Otani Yoshitsugu, at the foot of Mount Tengû, between Mount Sasao and Mount Matsuo.

Yoshitsugu and Mitsunari speculated on the possible arrival time of the Eastern forces, given the weather conditions and short distance from Akasaka. They worked out a strategy that would allow Ieyasu to be drawn into the middle of a four-sided box, and then squashed by loyalist samurai. If all went according to plan, some time after noon Ieyasu would be dead or captured, and Mitsunari would be the one to wield the power – in Hideyori's name, of course. Mitsunari must have smiled. Things were looking better and better. He was finally in the superior position. Their numbers seemed about the same, with about 80,000 men each in the field, but Mitsunari felt he was going to win.

As Mitsunari set up his command base on the slope of Mount Sasao the rain began to ease off and turned into a heavy mist. The roads were still soaked, though, and muddy. They had been churned up by thousands of

The plain of Sekigahara, seen from Ishida's position on Sasaoyama. Directly opposite is Mount Matsuo, on which Kobayakawa Hideaki set up camp. On the slopes to the right were the positions of Ukita Hideie and Konishi Yukinaga, and further to the right, the Shimazu.

feet and hooves, making it more and more difficult for rear forces to make headway. Despite the gloom, the Western Army was somehow able to take up positions.

Mitsunari personally led a force of 6,000 men. He divided his command into two, placing half in the nearby village of Oseki and keeping the other half with him. He ordered a moat dug, and erected two rows of palisades in front, giving command over them to Shima Sakon and Gamô Satoie (also known as Gamô Bitchû).

Sasaoyama, he knew, was critical to Ieyasu. It commanded the road, and if it was in Mitsunari's hands, Ieyasu would be unable to pass. Mitsunari hoped to be able to choke off the Nakasendô, and also the spur to the north, should Ieyasu try to escape that way. Whichever road the Tokugawa came for, Mitsunari was ready, and he had the Chôsokabe and Môri divisions beyond Mount Nangû to bring up behind Ieyasu to squash him.

The Toyotomi samurai would have been led by Hideyori had he been older, but at five years of age, he was in Osaka Castle with 'Uncle' Terumoto. In his place, the 2000-man Toyotomi division was led by Oda Nobutaka, Kishida Tadauji and Itô Morimasa. They took up positions just behind Mitsunari.

Shimazu Toyohisa and Yoshihiro each took half of their 1,500 men and formed into two units two ranks deep.

Last to arrive was Ukita Hideie at the head of 15,700 men. He took up a position in front of the southern foot of little Mount Tenman, setting up his forces in five rows.

The rest had already arrived and worked out their placement. The Western Army strategy was essentially like that of the battle formation referred to in old Chinese war texts as 'crane's wings'; the image was supposedly those of the wide-spread wings of a crane, ready to swoop down and enclose its prey.

The formation was complete by about 4.30 am. Ukita Hideie and Konishi Yukinaga settled in with Toda Shigemasa, Ôtani Yoshitsugu and Hiratsuka Tamehiro along the centre, between the Nakasendô and the road spur up to the north. On the right flank on Mount Matsuo, on the other side of the Nakasendô, were Kobayakawa Hideaki, Ôtani Yoshikatsu, Ogawa Suketada, the Toyotomi samurai and others. On their left flank, at the foot of Mount Sasao and south of the northern spur road, were Ishida Mitsunari, Shimazu Yoshihiro and his son Toyohisa, Gamô Bitchû, Shima Sakon and several others. Beyond Mount Nangû were Môri Hidemoto, Kikkawa Hiroie, Chôsakabe Morichika, Ankokuji Ekei and Natsuka Masaie.

Those who were able had long since settled down in their armour for an uncomfortable, wet nap.

Shortly before midnight, Ieyasu was informed that Mitsunari was on the move. As soon as he determined the direction, he understood the Western Army's plans. He sent word to his commanders and gave the order to make ready to march.

While the army prepared to move, Ieyasu gulped down a quick meal of hot rice porridge. He didn't know when the next chance to eat would come. He donned his armour, but refused a helmet, insisting that he had

no need, and putting on instead a simple brown silk crepe cap. He ordered the army to march, and pointed toward Sekigahara. Just before 2.00 am, with Fukushima Masanori in the lead position, the Eastern Army began to move slowly westward, slogging in the muddy road-bed of the Nakasendô, faces into the driving rain.

Ieyasu, taking a more direct route than Mitsunari, came into the valley about the same time as the latter. He chose to set up his command post on a hill called Mount Momokubari, at the north-western foot of Mount Nangû. His headquarters consisted of several bamboo poles ringed with camp curtains, and a rough mat floor. Ieyasu was not one for ostentatious displays, especially when there were more pressing matters. His personal command of 30,000 samurai set up directly in front of his large golden fan standard.

The mist was so thick that some time around 4.00 am the lead units of Fukushima Masanori's 6,000-man division actually came into contact with the lead units of Ukita Hideie. There was a brief scuffle, but the Eastern samurai pulled back into the mist and the incident ended as abruptly as it had begun.

The Eastern Army positioned itself along the Nakasendô and the southern road, both leading into the town, before dawn.

Several commanders took up a position between the Hokkoku-kaidô and Mount Sasao, opposite Mitsunari's barricades. They were Kuroda Nagamasa with his 5400 men, Tanaka Yoshimasa and his 3000, Hosokawa Tadaoki's 5,000-man division, Katô Yoshiaki's 3000 and Tsutsui Sadatsugu's 2850.

A string of positions was taken up behind Ieyasu on the Nakasendô in case the enemy tried to come up behind them on the road. Ieyasu had extracted Môri promises not to enter the battle, but he wasn't taking any chances.

The rest of his command took their places behind and around the front lines set up by Fukushima Masanori and those opposite Mitsunari.

Though exact numbers are impossible to come by, both sides were fielding roughly 85,000 men. Some sources have estimated that as many as 250,000 samurai were in the field that day. While this may be an accurate representation of the forces of both sides, they were not all present at Sekigahara; tens of thousands were occupied elsewhere in castle sieges.

Ieyasu pointed out to his commanders the great number of fires of the enemy burning on the mountainsides, commenting that he could easily smash them. Perhaps they looked at the fires and remembered an old trick Ieyasu had once played on them. He'd taken clam shells and covered the floor of a small room with them, then asked his men to tell him how many were there. One said five hundred, another a thousand. Ieyasu laughed, as there were only three hundred. It was a lesson his men would remember on how easily numbers could be misjudged when in a confined area.

As the generals looked out into the gloom, seeing nothing but occasional pinpricks of light, they must have felt some anxiety. They could do nothing until the fog cleared but wait, and hope to rest.

In his journal, Ieyasu's attendant physician, Itasaka Hokusai, wrote, 'The fifteenth [sic]. Slight rain. Dense fog in the mountain valley. Can't see

LEFT *In a traditionally under-stated way, the site of Ishida's command post is marked by a simple obelisk, some banners with Ishida's crest, and a few placards bearing maps pointing out unit positions.*

ninety yards. Fog lifted briefly and could see two or three hundred yards; fog then grew dense again. Barely made out enemy banners. On horseback, Lord Ieyasu made out positions of Ishida Mitsunari, Konishi Yukinaga and Ôtani Yoshitsugu. Estimate distance at two and a half miles.

THE OPENING ATTACKS

The fog that had filled the valley suddenly burned off at 8.00 am. The two armies blinked and stared at each other for a few moments, probably surprised at their actual proximity. The distance between the leading units could be covered in a few minutes' run.

It is not clear who first gave the order to attack, but the first troops to move were 30 mounted warriors from the Eastern line. To a man they were clad in flame-red armour, head to foot, with tall, red banners waving from their backs. Even the shafts of their lances were lacquered red. They were Ii Naomasa's men, the vanguard of his feared 'Red Devils'– the shock troops. Naomasa himself led the charge, against Ukita Hideie's position, and the battle was engaged.

Naomasa was the escort for Ieyasu's fourth son, 20-year-old Matsudaira Tadayoshi, but this charge gave him the chance to break free and see action, rather than babysit.

The battle straddled the Nakasendô, now paved and no longer the most important road in the region. The white banners waving about halfway up Sasaoyama (left) bear the mon of Ishida Mitsunari and mark the site of his camp and command post. A narrow road leads to the site of the final, decisive conflict. On both sides are rice paddies; undoubtedly much the same terrain as existed at the time of the battle. The roads were only muddy footpaths then, and the entire ground was churned up.

Kani Saizô, the captain of the advance guard of Fukushima Masanori's troops, raised his lance and shouted, 'The lead position belongs to Lord Fukushima! No one may advance beyond us!'

The honour of the lead position in the attack had been granted to the Fukushima. However, for Naomasa this simply wasn't satisfactory. This was partly the old rivalry problem among generals, but also that this battle was ultimately a Tokugawa versus Toyotomi affair (even though Mitsunari was leading the opposition), and Masanori, though fighting for Ieyasu and the Eastern Army, had long been a close vassal of Toyotomi Hideyoshi's; Masanori owed a great deal to the late taikô. To Naomasa, it just wasn't proper for Masanori to lead the attack; that honour should go to a loyal Tokugawa vassal, so he took it upon himself to alter the order of battle.

Naomasa, riding by Kani Saizô, shouted out in response that he was on an 'inspection' with the young Lord Tadayoshi, that they were taking a look at the front lines to show the young man how the enemy had disposed itself, and that there was no intent to start a fight. It was a blatant falsehood, of course, but Naomasa was still ahead.

With the Ii advance already accomplished by Naomasa's fiat, Masanori's division had no choice but to close ranks with the rest of the Ii contingent and fall on Ukita Hideie.

SEKIGHARA, 0600, 21 OCTOBER 1600

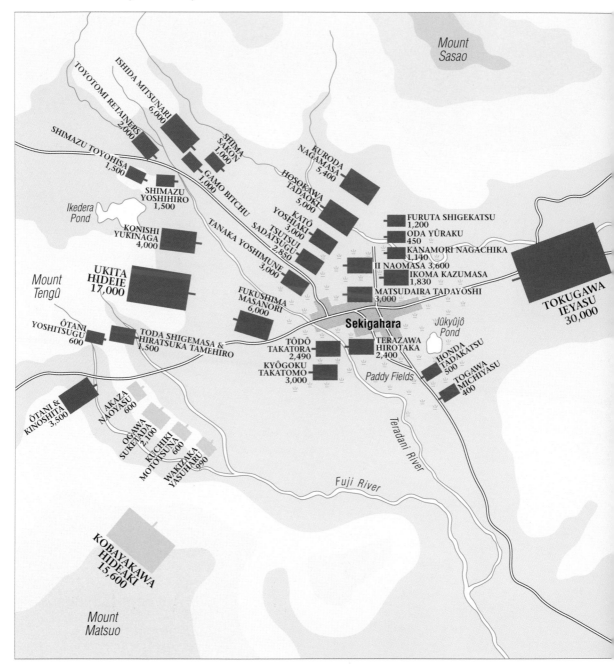

Ii Naomasa's initial charge, supported by the rest of his division, had hit so suddenly and fiercely that Ii's men briefly reached the Shimazu lines.

Both commanders must have realised then that their plans were to amount to little. There had been no time to work out grand-scale strategies. At best, plans had been makeshift, and at this point, the only strategy was to 'destroy the enemy'.

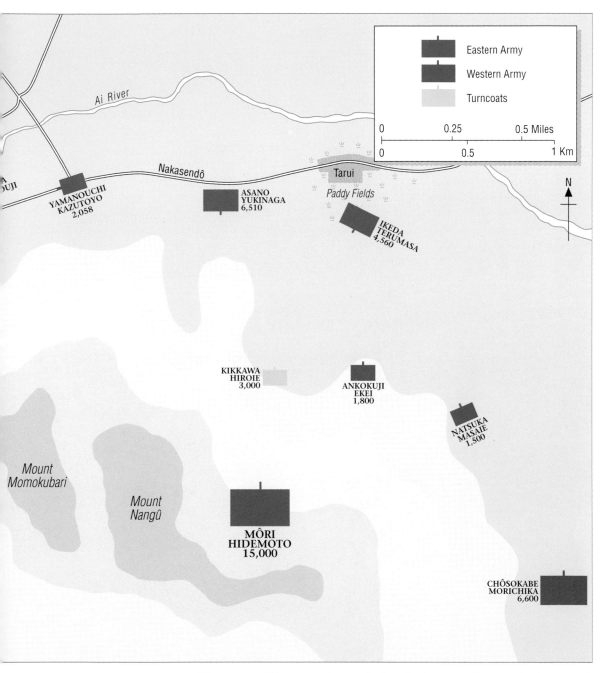

There was still some order to the battle, but not all troops had engaged. The arquebusiers of the Fukushima samurai poured lead into the Ukita position. The withering fire took a heavy toll of Hideie's men.

Kyôgoku Takatomo, Tôdô Takatora and Terazawa Hirotaka swept across the field and smashed into the massed ranks of Ôtani Yoshitsugu's troops almost immediately.

Reassured, Ieyasu moved forward, bringing his headquarters to about a mile from Mitsunari's position.

Nearly 20,000 men, under Kuroda Nagamasa, Tanaka Yoshimasa, Hosokawa Tadaoki, Katô Yoshiaki and Tsutsui Sadatsugu, made a direct charge on Mitsunari's command post. The fighting was hot and fierce, as they cut their way into the rings of defence Mitsunari had hurriedly created. Every inch of the way was bloody hand-to-hand work in the mud as the Easterners fought their way into Shima and Gamô's position.

Of all of the commanders in this attacking force, none wanted to kill Mitsunari personally as badly as Kuroda Nagamasa. All the old animosities from Korea welled up, along with the incident months before when Mitsunari had tried to assassinate Ieyasu. Nagamasa had been prevented from exacting revenge then, but this time he was determined. Nagamasa was not the only one. Mitsunari's forces must have fought surprisingly well to have held their position so strongly.

The Tokugawa gunners were putting heavy blanketing fire into the Ishida position as well, and they were shooting well that day. To support Nagamasa and the others in their attack, Togawa Michiyasu and Ikoma Kazumasa brought their arquebusiers up and fired right into the flank of Mitsunari's front lines, cutting a huge red swath out of it.

Shima Sakon, who'd come through the skirmish in Akasaka the day before without a scratch, fell, hit by enemy musket fire. He tried to regain

Sekigahara was a battle that hadn't exactly been planned; the troops were still arriving at 5.00 am. Nevertheless, some rude barricades of bamboo similar to those shown below had been erected in some areas to allow arquebusiers a safe area from which to fire, notably in front of Ishida Mitsunari's position. (Sekigahara Warland)

his position, but had to withdraw. Mitsunari ordered him to the rear, and he later died of his wounds.

Inspired, the Tokugawa samurai redoubled their efforts. Still Mitsunari refused to pull back. Instead he brought up five cannon and opened fire on the attacking Easterners. Considering that cannon in Japan were of little real effect, and primarily only of use against castle walls, this move was really for psychological effect.

It worked, and the Tokugawa began to slip back. Ishida sent a large force from his position against Tanaka Yoshimasa, but the forces of Katô Yoshiaki and Hosokawa Tadaoki regrouped and struck them from both sides forcing Mitsunari's men back into their defensive positions.

On the other side of Mount Nangû, Asano Yukinaga, observing that the battle had begun, led his 6510 Eastern samurai in a hard charge right into Natsuka Masaie. Chôsokabe and the other Western commanders, suddenly struck by doubt, stood and watched as the Asano troops tore into Natsuka's. The Môri, on the mountainside, waited for Kikkawa Hiroie to order them into action. He remained passive.

On both sides of the mountain the dull crackle of volley upon volley of arquebus fire filled the air, as both sides fired into whatever positions presented themselves. Over the popping of the matchlocks, the shouts and yells of the living merged with the screams of the injured and dying to fill the valley and echo back and forth.

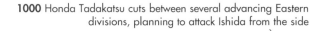

1000 Honda Tadakatsu cuts between several advancing Eastern divisions, planning to attack Ishida from the side

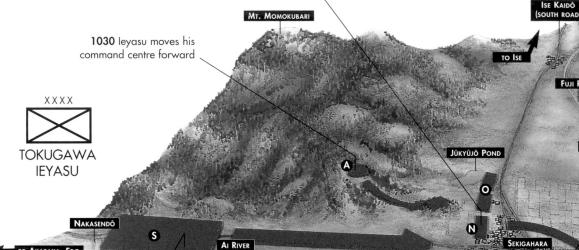

1030 Ieyasu moves his command centre forward

MT. MOMOKUBARI

ISE KAIDÔ (SOUTH ROAD)

TO ISE

FUJI RIVER

TERANDI

JÛKYÛJÔ POND

XXXX

TOKUGAWA IEYASU

SEKIGAHARA

NAKASENDÔ

TO AKASAKA, EDO

AI RIVER

1015 Ieyasu's main body is brought forward

0930 Furuta and Oda cut around behind several Eastern divisions and assume positions opposite Konishi Yukinaga

MARUYAMA

0830 Several Eastern generals, united in their hatred of Ishida Mitsunari, lead a grouped charge on his front defenses; pallisades erected and guarded by the men of Gamô Bitchû and Shima Sakon

EASTERN ARMY
A Tokugawa Ieyasu
B Ii Naomasa
C Matsudaira Tadayoshi
D Fukushima Masanori
E Kuroda Nagamasa
F Hosokawa Tadaoki
G Katô Yoshiaki
H Tsutsui Sadatsugu
I Tanaka Yoshimune
J Furuta Shigekatsu
K Oda Yûraku
L Kanamori Nagachika
M Ikoma Kazumasa
N Honda Tadakatsu
O Togawa Michiyasu
P Tôdô Takatora
Q Kyôgoku Takatomo
R Terazawa Hirotaka
S Tokugawa main body

WESTERN ARMY
1 Ishida Mitsunari
2 Toyotomi Retainers
3 Shimazu Toyohisa
4 Shimazu Yoshihiro
5 Shima Sakon
6 Gamô Bitchû
7 Konishi Yukinaga
8 Ukita Hideie
9 Ôtani Yoshitsugu
10 Toda Shigemasa
    & Hiratsuka Tamehiro
11 Ôtani Yoshikatsu
    & Kinoshita Terufusa

TURNCOATS
12 Kobayakawa Hideaki
13 Akaza Naoyasu
14 Ogawa Suketada
15 Kuchiki Mototsuna
16 Wakizaka Yasuharu

0800 The fog lifts and Ii Naomasa leads a charge onto the Western position, cutting in front of Fukushima Masanori and the Eastern vanguard

0800 Fukushima Masanori's men, not to be outdone, attack Ukita Hideie's position en masse

MT. MATSUO

X X

KOBAYAKAWA
HIDEAKI

12

16

15

14

13

9

8

MT. TENGŪ

7

11

10

TO KYŌTO, OSAKA

XXXX

ISHIDA
MITSUNARI

0900 Tôdô and Kyôgoku race across the field and meet the Ôtani forces descending Mt. Tengû

IKEDERA POND

3

4

HOKKOKU KAIDO
(NORTHERN ROAD)

2

TO WAKASA

1

N

SEKIGAHARA

21 October 1600, 0800–1100,
as seen from the north-west.
The fog lifts. Leading a sudden charge past his
own army's vanguard, Ii Naomasa, one of
Ieyasu's loyal commanders, starts the battle

One of the samurai, Ota Gyûichi, later wrote of the morning phase of the battle, 'Ally and foe pushed against each other. The musketfire and the shouts echoed from the heavens and shook the earth. The black smoke rose, making the day as night.'

Ôtani Yoshitsugu, Mitsunari's old friend, was locked in battle with the forces of Tôdô Takatora and Kyôgoku Takatomo, while Konishi Yukinaga's men were engaged in hand-to-hand combat with those of Oda Yûraku and Terazawa Hirotaka.

In all the battle, no place was more chaotic than the scene of the struggle between Fukushima Masanori and Ukita Hideie. It was hard going, and the battleline moved back and forth as if the desperately fighting samurai were but waves, washing up on a beach, and then receding only to return once more. Fukushima would push deep into the Western lines, only to have Western lancers drive him back, and it would begin again.

THE MORNING WEARS ON

At nearly 10.00 am, when the battle had been raging for nearly two hours, Ieyasu decided to move his command centre forwards again, to about half a mile from Mitsunari's position.

Although outwardly Ieyasu seemed certain of success, his attendant physician recorded a disturbing incident that casts a new light onto his demeanour and his state of mind. Just before departing for the new position, a retainer named Nonomura Shirozaemon dared to try to mount his horse before Ieyasu. This breach of protocol so enraged Ieyasu that he drew his sword and struck at Shirozaemon, injuring him. Shirozaemon fled, but Ieyasu was so angry that he struck the bannerpole of a page standing nearby, cutting it cleanly in two.

Ieyasu's rage was partly due to nerves. This was his life's climactic battle. The enemy had some 80,000 men in the field, but of them, so far only about 35,000 – Ishida, Ukita, Ôtani and Konishi – had engaged. What about the rest of Mitsunari's alliance?

All this time, the Shimazu had not moved. Even when threatened by an Ii advance at the onset of the battle, their line had never wavered one way or the other.

To Mitsunari's surprise and anger, old Shimazu Yoshihiro, who had been ready and raring to fight before the battle, had just sat there and watched the first series of attacks and counterattacks, even when the attacking Tokugawa coalition of Kuroda Nagamasa, Tanaka Yoshimasa, Hosokawa Tadaoki, Katô Yoshiaki and Tsutsui Sadatsugu nearly reached the palisades by Mitsunari's position.

Baffled, Mitsunari sent word to the Shimazu, inviting them forward, but the messenger insulted the proud Shimazu lord by failing to get off his horse before delivering his message. Mitsunari got no reply. Neither did Yoshihiro move forward.

Mitsunari finally jumped on his horse to go to Yoshihiro and personally order him into action. He galloped over to the Shimazu position, and sought out Yoshihiro.

Ukita Hideie (d. 1662) was a talented general, but his forces were no match for the Eastern juggernaut that descended on his and Konishi Yukinaga's position. After the battle, his death sentence was commuted, and he was allowed to shave his head and go into exile. He died at over 90 years of age, the oldest (and last) of the Sekigahara generals.

The older man drew himself up and stared at Mitsunari. 'In this battle,' he said, 'each unit must look to its own affairs and fight its own battles with all its might. There is no time to be concerned with the affairs of others in front, behind or on either flank.'

The effect of this response on Mitsunari's plans can only be guessed at. He had no choice but to trust that Yoshihiro would join the battle at some point, whenever he deemed the time was right.

Perhaps the root of this reproof was a slight Yoshihiro had suffered the night before, in Ogaki Castle, when his views on strategy had been rebuffed by Mitsunari, and he had gone unheard. Now Mitsunari would suffer the consequences of that insult.

Mitsunari returned to his own position to ascertain the course of battle and see what changes he would need to make for the next phase. It would now have to depend on Kobayakawa Hideaki and the Môri clan on the other side of Mount Nangû.

The loyalists had been struck hard, but they began to regroup, and under the firm leadership of Ukita Hideie with the main body, they were able to begin slowly to drive the Tokugawa forces back.

For a while Hideie was able to hold his own. He looked as if he was doing too well, in fact. Mitsunari's plan had been for him to hold Ieyasu's men, while Kobayakawa Hideaki fell on them from one side, he from the other, and the Môri contingents came up from behind. Boxed in, the Tokugawa would be destroyed; but Hideie had pushed the Tokugawa almost beyond a possible flank attack from Hideaki.

Konishi Yukinaga's men were forced farther and farther back under the onslaught of the Tokugawa forces. Otani Yoshikatsu was holding his own, and even made some gains, but it was close fighting.

It was now 11.00 am. The field was a chaotic swarm of banners of all colours, with crests of dozens of lords and dozens of units. Men fought and fell by the hundred.

Mitsunari surveyed the field from his vantage on Mount Sasao, and decided that the time was right for an all-out push. This would be the deciding action that would crush the Tokugawa.

Hideie's men were being pushed again, so Mitsunari ordered the signal fire lit to bring Kobayakawa Hideaki and his 15,000-man division into the

EAST OF MT. NANGÛ,
1000, 21 OCTOBER 1600

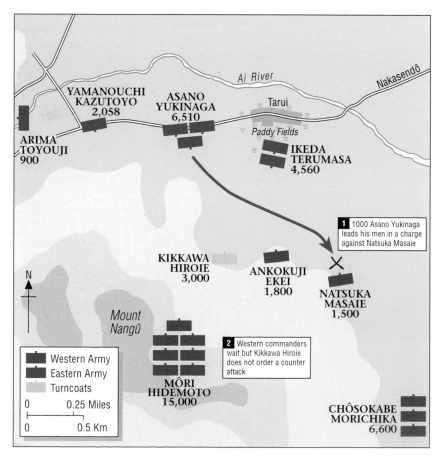

ABOVE *Officers had better quality armour than the rank and file, of course. This man wears a hishinui dô lacquered over in deep red. His banner is also red. He could be intended to represent an officer of Ii Naomasa's Red Devils. A hishinui dô is a cuirass of solid lames held together with small crossed lacing instead of the usual rivets. (Japan Costume Museum)*

RIGHT *Armours such as these were far more common at Sekigahara. Although a replica deliberately 'dirtied down' to give the impression of age, it is typical of those worn by samurai in the thousands. The simple riveted solid cuirass has a hinge under the left arm, and tied closed under the right. It is called an okegawa dô, or 'tub-sided cuirass' after the shape. The crest, a large butterfly, is that of the Ikeda clan, who fought under Ieyasu. (Nagakute Battlefield Museum)*

fight. He would turn the tide of the battle once and for all. Mitsunari watched and waited.

When he saw no Kobayakawa banners start down the mountainside opposite his position, Mitsunari was stunned. First Shimazu Yoshihiro had refused to move, now Hideaki. He signalled frantically but to no avail. Who would defy him next, he must have wondered. He could not have guessed that the entire Môri clan had abandoned him.

On their own side of Mount Nangû, Ankokuji Ekei and Natsuka Masaie saw the smoke of the signal fires. They knew it was the signal for Hideaki to sweep down the mountain, and it was also the signal for them to strike; but Kikkawa Hiroie never moved either. They sent word to him, asking what was wrong, but he sent no replies other than that he was busy eating, and please to leave him alone. They couldn't move without him, so they had to sit and wait, listening to the din of a battle they couldn't see and wondering who had the upper hand.

From his position behind and to the right of Ukita Hideie, Ôtani Yoshitsugu also saw the signal fire, and knew what it meant. He was not as surprised as Mitsunari, having suspected some possible treachery on Hideaki's part. Pressed as he was by Tôdo Takatora and Kyôgoku Takatomo (son of the defender of Otsu Castle), he sent messengers up to

The fighting was intense, wet and muddy. The niceties of calling out names and stations and demanding one-on-one combat, common in the ancient days, was no more. (Sekigahara Warland)

Hideaki's camp entreating him to come down the mountain, but this also failed to produce any action. Even Konishi Yukinaga sent word up the mountain to Hideaki, pleading with him to support his position. Hideaki never budged.

Ieyasu was watching from his own position, and noted that while the Kobayakawa were not descending upon his forces, they weren't descending on the Western Army either. What was the cause for the hesitation, he wondered.

As a brief side note, an amusing anecdote illustrates the importance samurai – especially lords – placed on politeness and comportment, even during the heat of battle. Ieyasu sent a messenger, Yamagami Goemon, to Kuroda Nagamasa to ascertain whether Kobayakawa Hideaki would indeed come over to their side. Goemon galloped over to Nagamasa, and shouted, 'Kôshu, Kôshu! Do you know, will Lord Hideaki join us or not?' (Kôshu was the name of Nagamasa's fief, the province of Kai. This was roughly equivalent to a messenger calling out to General Kitchener, 'Broome, hey, Broome!')

Nagamasa replied, 'You know as much as I do. Even if he doesn't join us, we can cut through Ishida and eliminate Kobayakawa's men and Ukita's easily. Now if you don't mind, I have my men to look to!' After the messenger had left, Nagamasa turned to his lieutenant and shook his head in disgust. 'That man has no understanding of what manners are. Yes, we are in combat, but there is no cause to neglect etiquette. How rude, calling out "Kôshu, Kôshu!" like that!'

Meanwhile, Kuroda Nagamasa had sent Okubo Inosuke up the mountain. Inosuke grabbed Hideaki's advisor, Hiraoka Yorikatsu, by the

1200 Ieyasu moves his command centre forward once again

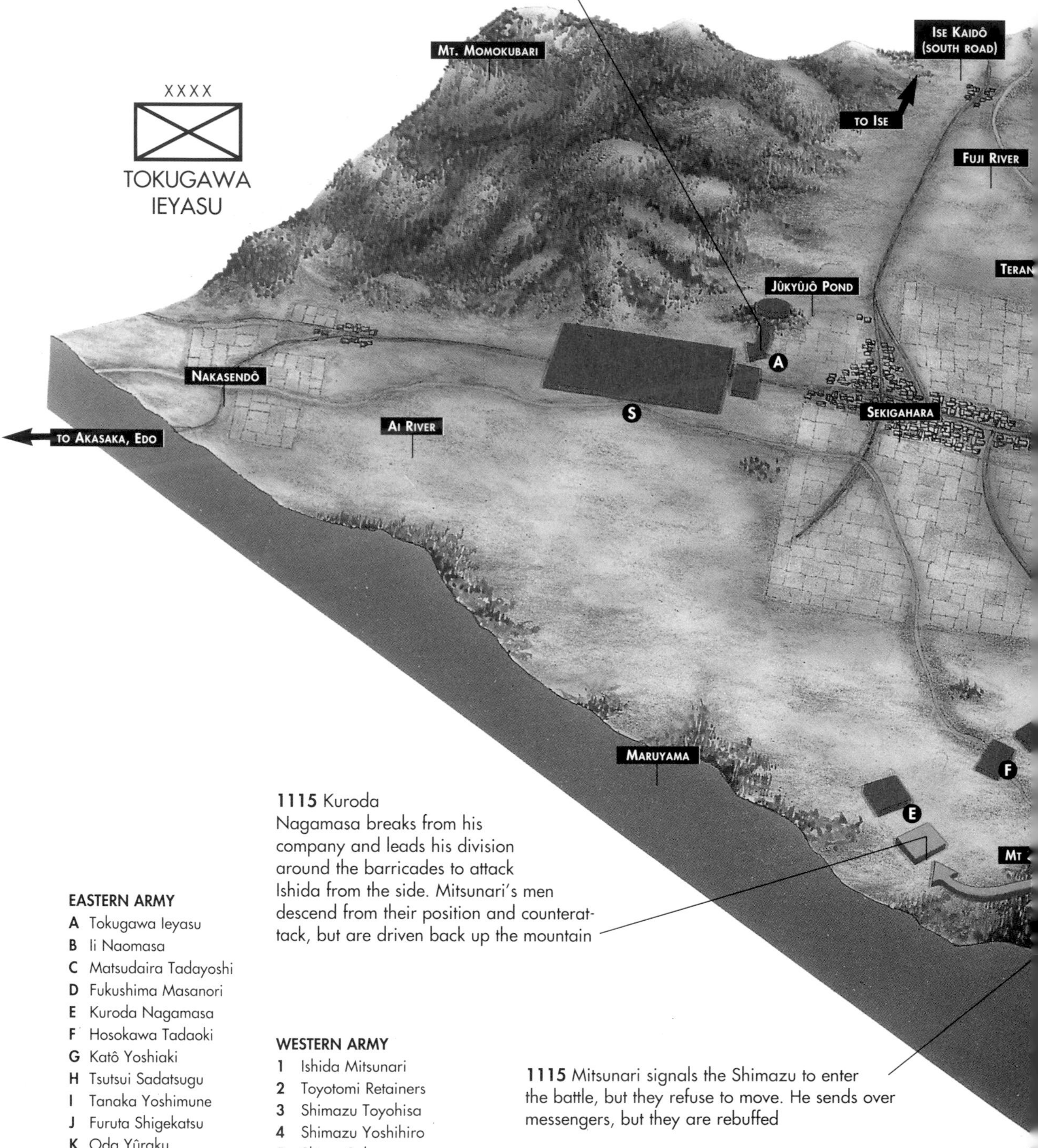

MT. MOMOKUBARI

ISE KAIDÔ (SOUTH ROAD)

TO ISE

FUJI RIVER

TERAN

JÛKYÛJÔ POND

A

NAKASENDÔ

S

AI RIVER

TO AKASAKA, EDO

SEKIGAHARA

TOKUGAWA IEYASU

XXXX

MARUYAMA

F

E

MT

1115 Kuroda Nagamasa breaks from his company and leads his division around the barricades to attack Ishida from the side. Mitsunari's men descend from their position and counterattack, but are driven back up the mountain

1115 Mitsunari signals the Shimazu to enter the battle, but they refuse to move. He sends over messengers, but they are rebuffed

1130 Honda Tadakatsu and Togawa Michiyasu engage Konishi Yukinaga

EASTERN ARMY
A Tokugawa Ieyasu
B Ii Naomasa
C Matsudaira Tadayoshi
D Fukushima Masanori
E Kuroda Nagamasa
F Hosokawa Tadaoki
G Katô Yoshiaki
H Tsutsui Sadatsugu
I Tanaka Yoshimune
J Furuta Shigekatsu
K Oda Yûraku
L Kanamori Nagachika
M Ikoma Kazumasa
N Honda Tadakatsu
O Togawa Michiyasu
P Tôdô Takatora
Q Kyôgoku Takatomo
R Terazawa Hirotaka
S Tokugawa main body

WESTERN ARMY
1 Ishida Mitsunari
2 Toyotomi Retainers
3 Shimazu Toyohisa
4 Shimazu Yoshihiro
5 Shima Sakon
6 Gamô Bitchû
7 Konishi Yukinaga
8 Ukita Hideie
9 Ôtani Yoshitsugu
10 Toda Shigemasa
   & Hiratsuka Tamehiro
11 Ôtani Yoshikatsu
   & Kinoshita Terufusa

TURNCOATS
12 Kobayakawa Hideaki
13 Akaza Naoyasu
14 Ogawa Suketada
15 Kuchiki Mototsuna
16 Wakizaka Yasuharu

1100 The bulk of Ôtani Yoshitsugu's forces are engagaed with those of Tôdô Takatora and Kyôgoku Takatomo

1200 Despite Ishida's repeated signal to engage the Eastern forces, Kobayakawa Hideaki fails to move. On the other side of Mount Nangû, Kikkawa Hideaki observes the signal to attack but holds his position

X X

KOBAYAKAWA HIDEAKI

1130 Suspecting something, divisions of the Western army under Ôtani Yoshitsugu's overall command reposition themselves to observe the Kobayakawa troops

MT. MATSUO

12

16

15

14

13

10

11

TO KYÔTO, OSAKA →

M

R

Q

P

9

D

MT. TENGÛ

8

O

N

7

C

IKEDERA POND

B

3

4

1100 Ukita and Fukushima's division are engaged in fierce fighting

1130 Terazawa Hirotaka leads his forces for a rear assault on Ukita Hideie, who is already engaged frontally with Fukushima Masanori

1130 Ii Naomasa and Matsudaira Tadayoshi assault the Shimazu position. The Shimazu defend, and finally around noon counterattack

HOKKOKU KAIDO (NORTHERN ROAD)

2

TO WAKASA →

X X X X

ISHIDA MITSUNARI

N

SEKIGAHARA

21 October 1600, 1100–1200, as seen from the north-west. The Western command begins to come apart. Despite repeated signals, orders and finally requests, whole divisions fail to engage the Eastern forces

A teppô-tai, or matchlock corps, under the command of Katô Yoshiakira prepares to fire. There were thousands of matchlocks in use that day, and most commanders had several contingents of arque-busiers. (Sekigahara Warland)

skirtplates on his armour, and with his free hand thrust a short sword up against the advisor's abdomen. 'The battle has already begun,' he said. 'Now is the time for either victory or defeat. There is some doubt about your intent to change sides. If you have lied to Lord Kuroda [about your intentions], I'll run this through you right here!'

HIDEAKI'S DEFECTION

Ieyasu, like Mitsunari, was made anxious by Hideaki's inaction. Many historians have commented that as he watched Hideaki's position, he chewed nervously on his fingernails. Ieyasu was determined to force Hideaki's hand, so he directed a detachment of arquebusiers to fire on the Kobayakawa position, just behind Hideaki.

The musket fire seemed to awaken and galvanise Hideaki, who leapt up and shouted, 'Our target is Otani Yoshitsugu!' Mounting his horse, he ordered his 15,000 men to charge down the mountainside right into the flank of Otani Yoshitsugu's men.

It was shortly after noon. Otani Yoshitsugu suffered from leprosy, and was badly disabled and nearly blind. He commanded his division from a special litter he was being carried in. His body was failing him, but his mind was as sharp as ever. Yoshitsugu had been prepared for anything, anticipating treachery the moment he realised that Hideaki was delaying coming into the battle. Half his men promptly wheeled right and began fighting on his flank.

Yoshitsugu had placed the two combined divisions (Toda Shigemasa and Hiratsuka Tamehiro, and Ôtani Yoshikatsu and Kinoshita Yoritsugu) on his flanks to guard against such an eventuality. Unfortunately, however, they were already engaged in front by forces from the Eastern Army; they were

Heads being carried in for viewing after the battle. After they were taken, the heads were usually washed and prepared for display, with name tags attached to their queues or ears. Such niceties may have been over-looked after Sekigahara, considering the number of Western heads taken, some 40,000. (Sekigahara Warland)

Ôtani Yoshitsugu (1559-1600) was a good strategist and an able general. He commanded several units in his wing, keeping direct command on only 600 crack troops. He suffered from leprosy, and was forced to command from a special litter. He had anticipated a possible defection by Kobayakawa Hideaki, but he was overcome by sheer numbers and so had a retainer kill him and hide his head so the enemy would have no prize. From a contemporary portrait.

under attack by divisions commanded by Kyôgoku Takatsugu, Tôdô Takatora and Oda Yûraku.

Yoshitsugu's buffer was outnumbered, and one by one the commanders were slain and their men routed. Matters worsened when Western division commanders Wakizaka Yasuharu, Kuchiki Mototsuna, Ogawa Suketada and Akaza Naoyasu followed Hideaki's lead, charged down Mount Sasao and struck at their erstwhile allies, the samurai of Ôtani Yoshitsugu.

Yoshitsugu knew his cause was lost and his position was being over-run. He saw too that retreat and escape was out of the question for a man in his condition. Yoritsugu leaned out of his litter and requested a retainer, Yuasa Gorô, to kill him and hide his head so the enemy wouldn't get it as a trophy. Weeping, Gorô complied with his master's last wish as a ring of Otani samurai held the turncoats at bay. After slaying his lord, Gorô removed Yoshitsugu's head and ran and hid it in the bloody, mud–caked undergrowth. Gorô's final duty was yet to be done; surrounded by the din of battle, he sat down on a rise in the muddy grass and opened his belly. He had done well. Yoshitsugu's head was never found.

The Kobayakawa cut cleanly through the remaining Ôtani troops, and supported with the other turncoats, fell on the Ukita and Konishi positions. Unlike Ôtani Yoshitsugu, neither Yukinaga nor Hideie had expected or prepared for treason, and they had no defences ready against this sudden onslaught from the rear.

73

1500 The Shimazu, in the confusion of a general rout, flee south. With Shimazu Toyohisa killed, Shimazu Yoshihiro leads their remaining troops over Mount Tengû and south skirting the valley. They will circle around the south of Mount Nangû, and contact the rearguard of the Môri and Chôsokabe troops there; the first news from the battle their allies hear will be of the loyalist defeat

MT. MOMOKUBARI

TO ISE

FUJI RIVER

ISE KAIDÔ
(SOUTH ROAD)

XXXX

TOKUGAWA
IEYASU

JÛKYÛJÔ POND

TERAN

NAKASENDÔ

AI RIVER

SEKIGAHARA

TO AKASAKA, EDO

A S

1400 Ieyasu declares the day his and sends out support troops to begin the mopping up

MARUYAMA

F

E

MT S

1230 Gamô Bitchû and Shima Sakon's units are crushed and give way, melting back into the Ishida forces

1400 With his commanders in retreat and his own command in danger of being overrun, Ishida accepts defeat and escapes into the mountains

EASTERN ARMY
A Tokugawa Ieyasu
B Ii Naomasa
C Matsudaira Tadayoshi
D Fukushima Masanori
E Kuroda Nagamasa
F Hosokawa Tadaoki
G Katô Yoshiaki
H Tsutsui Sadatsugu
I Tanaka Yoshimune
J Furuta Shigekatsu
K Oda Yûraku
L Kanamori Nagachika
M Ikoma Kazumasa
N Honda Tadakatsu
O Togawa Michiyasu
P Tôdô Takatora
Q Kyôgoku Takatomo
R Terazawa Hirotaka
S Tokugawa main body

WESTERN ARMY
1 Ishida Mitsunari
2 Toyotomi Retainers
3 Shimazu Toyohisa
4 Shimazu Yoshihiro
5 Shima Sakon (destroyed)
6 Gamô Bitchû (destroyed)
7 Konishi Yukinaga
8 Ukita Hideie
9 Ôtani Yoshitsugu
10 Toda Shigemasa
    & Hiratsuka Tamehiro
11 Ôtani Yoshikatsu
    & Kinoshita Terufusa

TURNCOATS
12 Kobayakawa Hideaki
13 Akaza Naoyasu
14 Ogawa Suketada
15 Kuchiki Mototsuna
16 Wakizaka Yasuharu

XXXX

ISHIDA
MITSUNARI

1300 Inspired by Kobayakawa, four more Western generals defect and fall on the Ôtani positions, causing general confusion. The defecting samurai receive support from Eastern samurai coming up on the Ôtani position

1215 Kobayakawa Hideaki suddenly sweeps down Mount Matsuo onto the rear units of Ôtani Yoshitsugu, commanded by Ôtani Yoshikatsu, Kinoshita Terufusa, Toda Shigemasa and Hiratsuka Tamehiro. After destroying the remaining forces (Ôtani Yoshitsugu is killed), they continue forward, falling on Ukita Hideie's position from behind

KOBAYAKAWA
HIDEAKI

MT. MATSUO

12
15 14 13
16
Q 11
P 10
D
9
K M R
O 8
L
N MT. TENGŪ
7
I C
B 3
4
2

IKEDERA POND

TO KYÔTO, OSAKA →

1315
Already heavily engaged, Ukita Hideie is set upon by Togawa Michiyoshi, who passes up striking at Konishi's line in favour of attacking Ukita. When hit from the rear by the advancing Kobayakawa samurai, his command begins to disintegrate. Before he can make a suicide charge at Kobayakawa Hideaki, his men force him to flee

1330 Konishi, sorely beset, is also the target of Hideaki's advance. Seeing no other option, he flees into the mountains

1330 The Shimazu, sorely pressed, are barely able to hold their own. They are retreating when Ii Naomasa, spearheading the assault on them, is struck by musketfire and abandons the field. In another hour, they will finally be forced to retreat south and around Mounts Momokubari and Nangû

HOKKOKU KAIDO
(NORTHERN ROAD) TO WAKASA →

N

SEKIGAHARA

21 October 1600, 1200–1500, as seen from the north-west. Treason in the Western ranks spells doom for the loyalist cause. Those Western commanders not slain are finally forced to flee. Ieyasu claims the day

Still, even before Konishi Yukinaga and Ukita Hideie were attacked by the turncoats, it had become obvious to the main body of the army that there was treason in the ranks, and this had bred confusion. Confronted by the enemy on both sides, the Western front began to crumble.

Hideie vowed to take Kobayakawa Hideaki's head personally before leaving the field; he turned to attempt to fight his way through his own men to where Hideaki's men were fighting. His lieutenants held him back, and escorted him to safety in the rear. The battle was nearing its conclusion, so Hideie followed Konishi Yukinaga in a desperate flight up into Mount Ibuki. For them the battle was over.

The Shimazu were finally engaged by the relentless Ii, and Shimazu Yoshihiro saw his nephew, Toyohisa, fall under the onslaught of Naomasa's men. He too saw that his only option was to escape, so with his remaining 80 or so men, Yoshihiro began to cut his way out.

The battle was almost over, but Naomasa didn't want to let Yoshihiro get away. This was no blood-fever or berserk rage; for Naomasa, Yoshihiro was nothing more than an enemy commander, and until the fighting stopped, his duty was to cut off every possible head of the Western hydra. He regrouped briefly and then threw his full strength into a further attack. Yoshihiro's remaining forces tried to hold Naomasa off but with little success, until a few arquebusiers were able to get off a final volley. Naomasa was too close for his own good; struck in the shoulder by a musket ball, he wheeled and nearly fell from his horse. It was pure luck on the part of the Shimazu, but it forced Naomasa to withdraw from the fray, and his key command followed him, abandoning the Shimazu to their frantic retreat. When Naomasa died 18 months later, at the age of 42, his death was attributed to the wounds he received at Sekigahara.

Konishi Yukinaga and Ukita Hideie had made a slight advance on the Tokugawa position, so when Hideaki's men struck, they had done so virtually behind the Shimazu position. Seeing any avenue of retreat to the west closed off, the Shimazu were forced to retreat to the south, around Mount Nangû.

Kikkawa Hiroie, in the vanguard of the Môri forces, with his 3000 men beyond Mount Nangu, refused to move. His inaction forced Môri Hidemoto, who was behind him further up the mountain, to do likewise, and he kept his 15,000 men out of the action as well. Everyone could hear the battle raging, and though Ankokuji Ekei and Chôsokabe Morichika wanted to advance, they were prevented from doing so.

The Shimazu troops, fleeing south and east behind Mount Nangû, ran across the rearguards of Chôsokabe Morichika's division. For a moment it was chaos, with Morichika's men thinking they had been flanked. Then

By all accounts, Kobayakakawa Hideaki wore a helmet such as this during the battle of Sekigahara. It is a variation on the eboshi-nari kabuto, or court cap-shaped helmet. A more drastic example was that worn by Katô Kiyomasa, which stood a good two feet or more tall. (Gifu Castle)

Ieyasu, in his camp after the end of the battle, has begun to view the heads of the enemy slain in battle. Viewing the taken heads was an important part of the battle process, affording a certain cold finality among other things. The opposing commanders could be praised or derided, and based on the attitude of the face, good or bad luck was believed to be manifested. (Sekigahara Warland)

the rearguards recognised the banners of the Shimazu. The fleeing Shimazu told their allies that the cause was lost. Word spread quickly through the Chôsokabe regiments, and thence to the rest of the forces on the east of Mount Nangû. They were too late; if they had entered the battle, things would have been different. Perhaps there was still a chance, but Kikkawa Hiroie's inaction still prevented Môri Hidemoto from coming forward. The battle was over.

The loyalist forces east of Mount Nangû began to scatter. The rout had begun.

Mitsunari, with many of his seasoned commanders slain or in retreat, also chose the only option he could. With a handful of retainers, he fled up the mountain roads heading north, leaving the field to Ieyasu.

The Western armies began to retreat en masse.

The battle was over but for the mopping up, and it wasn't even 2.00 pm. Less than 12 hours before, Mitsunari had anticipated this day would see him master of Japan. Instead, Ieyasu was the master, and Mitsunari was fleeing for his life.

One of the many ironies of this battle is that there were enough reserves on the slopes of Mount Nangû to have secured a victory for the loyalist cause, even with the Kobayakawa defection. The fact that the Môri leader was not inclined to help Mitsunari, of course, rendered the situation academic.

Pockets of enemy forces were still fighting as they withdrew, and the Shimazu were still on their way around Mount Nangû, but at 2.00 pm Ieyasu declared the battle over.

THE END OF THE BATTLE

In his new camp Ieyasu finally put on the helmet that he had eschewed all night and all morning. 'After victory,' he said, 'tighten the cords of your helmet.' Whether he was the first to utter this axiom is uncertain, but the meaning – don't allow yourself to be overconfident when you think

you've won – is clear, and it is now a well-known saying in Japan.

He sat down, surrounded by his officers and advisors, and ordered the viewing of heads to be prepared. Meanwhile, his generals began to arrive, bringing word of their commands.

Kuroda Nagamasa came first. Ieyasu stood and warmly greeted Nagamasa, saying, 'Today's victory is entirely due to your loyalty and effort. As long as my house flourishes, the Kuroda shall want for nothing.' And he took a valuable short sword by a revered smith and placed it in Nagamasa's sash with his own hands.

Nagamasa was followed by Honda Tadakatsu and Fukushima Masanori, both of whom Ieyasu praised highly. The badly wounded Ii Naomasa was helped in, accompanied by Ieyasu's son Tadayoshi, who had performed bravely that day. Ieyasu called for bandages and personally attended to the wound of his old friend, while Ii told him how well his son had performed on the field. 'But,' he concluded, 'hawks of fine stock always turn out well.'

Ieyasu returned the compliment, remarking that a good trainer is still necessary, no matter how well-bred the hawk.

Shortly after, Kobayakawa Hideaki walked silently into the encampment, and threw himself down prostrate before Ieyasu. He apologised for the Fushimi Castle siege, in which he'd participated under orders from Ishida, and asked that in return for that mistake he be allowed to lead the attack on Sawayama. Ieyasu consented, and thanked him for his efforts.

Much later, after the heads had been viewed and counted, Hidetada arrived. At first Ieyasu wouldn't see him, but late that evening he finally admitted his errant son into his presence. Ieyasu didn't mince words. Hidetada had nearly cost him the battle, and it would be a long time before Ieyasu would be able to·forget that horrible lapse of judgement.

THE AFTERMATH

After the battle, Ieyasu lost little time securing the victory he had won on the field. His initial goal had been the Ishida home castle, Sawayama, so on 22 October he continued the campaign by directing his forces at Sawayama. Kobayakawa Hideaki was given the honour of leading the attack, and at the head of 15,000 men – principally made up of those who had defected to Ieyasu's banner – he set upon the castle.

A demoralised Ishida Masazumi, Mitsunari's brother, in command of the castle, capitulated and committed suicide on the second day, his castle in flames.

RETRIBUTION

Ieyasu and Môri Terumoto exchanged a flurry of letters as Ieyasu approached Ôsaka. The victorious Tokugawa Ieyasu could forgive many things. He could forgive an opponent for bearing arms against him. He could even forgive an assassination attempt. One thing he could not forgive was Terumoto's lack of action. As one who had accepted the position of commander-in-chief of the loyalist forces, Terumoto had been honour-bound to support the cause. If he hadn't wanted to fight, he shouldn't have accepted the rank; so reasoned Ieyasu.

There was no need to humiliate the Môri clan, as their ability to resist was gone, but Ieyasu feigned ignorance of the agreements made with Kikkawa Hiroie. He began by displacing Terumoto from Ôsaka Castle, and then ordered him to turn over some of his more profitable fiefs to Hiroie. Hiroie was shocked; this had not been his motive for acting as he did. He had hoped to save the Môri clan, and felt that instead he had only brought about its ruin. Terumoto, whose estates produced 1.2 million koku, was reduced to fiefs yielding only 360,000.

Konishi Yukinaga turned himself in to fellow Christian daimyô Kuroda Nagamasa. He was offered the opportunity to commit seppuku, but he declined. As a devout Christian, suicide was not an option for him. Whatever else Yukinaga may have been, he considered himself a true Christian knight, and Dom Augustin – for such was he called by the missionaries – would die as one. It is interesting to note that Nagamasa refused to allow Yukinaga to meet with a priest as he requested.

Mitsunari and Ankokoji Ekei were both captured and duly handed over to Tokugawa samurai. As committed enemies of the Tokugawa, there was only one possible fate which could await them.

When Mitsunari, Yukinaga and Ankokuji Ekei were being escorted to the Kyoto execution grounds, a townsman offered them some persimmons to eat. Mitsunari, ever contrary, refused, saying that they would be bad for his digestion. Yukinaga wryly pointed out that, as they were to die in an hour, digestion should be the last thing on Mitsunari's mind. 'On the contrary,' Mitsunari replied, 'no matter what the situation, you can never know how things are going to come out.'

They were all beheaded at Kyôto's ancient execution site of Rokujô-ga-hara. For Mitsunari, the persimmons would have made no difference at all.

Ukita Hideie fled the battlefield and went into hiding in Satsuma, the home of the Shimazu. In his absence, his three-province fief of Okayama was taken and given away. In 1603 Shimazu Iehisa revealed his hiding place to Ieyasu, who promptly sentenced Hideie to death. After consideration, the shôgun instead sent him into permanent exile on the island of Hachijô-jima, near Izu. He died there in 1655 at the age of 84. He was the last to die of the lords who participated in the great battle.

Ieyasu had to be careful with how he dealt with the young Hideyori, however. There were many daimyô who had fought for Ieyasu who still owed a great deal to Hideyori's father, and they remembered their debts. For them, the war had been against Mitsunari, not Hideyori. Ieyasu installed Hideyori in Osaka Castle, and gave him the provinces of Settsu, Kawachi and Izumi, with a revenue of 650,000 koku.

In 1603 Ieyasu promised his six-year-old grand-daughter in marriage to Hideyori. In the same year, Emperor Go-Yôzei granted Ieyasu the prize he had sought for so long – the title of shôgun.

Twelve years later, on the flimsy pretext of having been insulted by a poor choice of wording on a temple bell Hideyori had ordered cast, Ieyasu once more assembled his army and laid siege to Osaka Castle. Many of the daimyô who had once supported the loyalist cause during the Sekigahara campaign now distinguished themselves in the destruction of the Toyotomi stronghold, which was burned to the ground. Hideyori committed suicide, and his clan and cause were no more.

The momo-nari, or peach-form, was a popular variation of helmet worn by those with the money to acquire better-quality materials. This example has horns and a gilt dragonfly crest (the dragonfly was called 'victory bug', and was therefore an auspicious symbol to the warrior class). (Yoroi no Kôzan-dô)

Yamanouchi Kazutoyo (1546-1605), who fought for Ieyasu at Sekigahara, wore a cuirass lacquered in an odd pattern of red with black 'drips'; and a gold axe embellished on his chest. Kazutoyo's was one of the more eccentrically decorated armours, as this modern replica attests. After the battle, Ieyasu rewarded him with the province of Tosa – worth over 240,000 koku. (Yoroi no Kôzan-dô)

Many Christian samurai took part in the battle, fighting in both armies. Their leaders probably wore nanban-gusoku (European – literally 'southern barbarian' – armours), gifts of European princes or priests, or even objects sold by foreign merchants. Most such armours were modified heavily to Japanese taste. (Yoroi no Kôzan-dô)

OTHER BATTLES, AUGUST–OCTOBER 1600

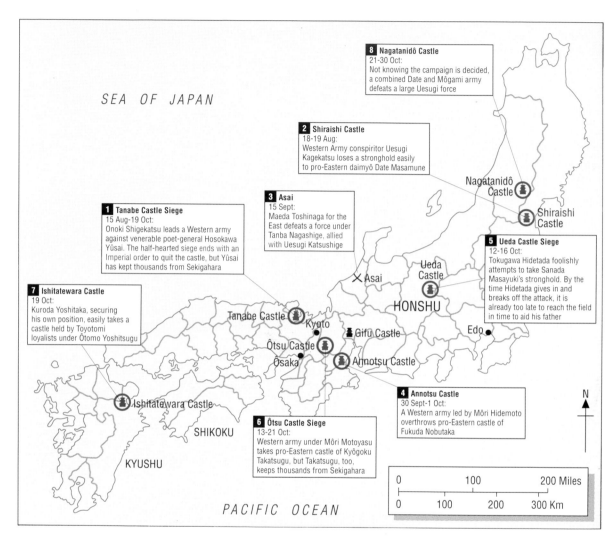

SEA OF JAPAN

8 Nagatanidô Castle
21–30 Oct:
Not knowing the campaign is decided, a combined Date and Môgami army defeats a large Uesugi force

2 Shiraishi Castle
18–19 Aug:
Western Army conspiritor Uesugi Kagekatsu loses a stronghold easily to pro-Eastern daimyô Date Masamune

1 Tanabe Castle Siege
15 Aug–19 Oct:
Onoki Shigekatsu leads a Western army against venerable poet-general Hosokawa Yûsai. The half-hearted siege ends with an Imperial order to quit the castle, but Yûsai has kept thousands from Sekigahara

3 Asai
15 Sept:
Maeda Toshinaga for the East defeats a force under Tanba Nagashige, allied with Uesugi Katsushige

5 Ueda Castle Siege
12–16 Oct:
Tokugawa Hidetada foolishly attempts to take Sanada Masayuki's stronghold. By the time Hidetada gives in and breaks off the attack, it is already too late to reach the field in time to aid his father

7 Ishitatewara Castle
19 Oct:
Kuroda Yoshitaka, securing his own position, easily takes a castle held by Toyotomi loyalists under Ôtomo Yoshitsugu

Nagatanidô Castle

Shiraishi Castle

Ueda Castle

HONSHU

Asai

Tanabe Castle
Kyoto

Ôtsu Castle

Ôsaka

Gifu Castle

Edo

Annotsu Castle

4 Annotsu Castle
30 Sept–1 Oct:
A Western army led by Môri Hidemoto overthrows pro-Eastern castle of Fukuda Nobutaka

Ishitatewara Castle

SHIKOKU

KYUSHU

6 Ôtsu Castle Siege
13–21 Oct:
Western army under Môri Motoyasu takes pro-Eastern castle of Kyôgoku Takatsugu, but Takatsugu, too, keeps thousands from Sekigahara

N

0		100		200 Miles
0	100	200	300 Km	

PACIFIC OCEAN

TO THE VICTOR THE SPOILS

To reward his supporters, Ieyasu took land from 90 families – 6.5 million koku in total. A great deal of the confiscated revenues went to Tokugawa family coffers, but many an ally and vassal was made wealthy for supporting his cause.

Ieyasu began to reapportion fiefs in earnest, giving more profitable territories to those who had supported him and removing those who had opposed him to less productive ones. Many erstwhile enemies were allowed to offer fealty and thereby retain some rank, but they would always be excluded from the Tokugawa circle of influence.

True to his word, Ieyasu rewarded Kobayakawa Hideaki, the young lord whose sudden defection had proved the turning point for the Eastern Army, with the fiefs of Bizen and Mimasaka, with a total revenue of

520,000 koku. Only two years after the battle, however, Hideaki died heirless at the age of 20, and the lands reverted to the shôgun.

Katô Kiyomasa, Hideyoshi's old vassal who had sided with Ieyasu, was rewarded with his old enemy Konishi Yukinaga's fief, the other half of the province of Higo (he already had the first half as his own fief), and saw his wealth rise to 520,000 koku. He was still loyal to the Toyotomi family, however. Eleven years later, after visiting Ieyasu, Kiyomasa suddenly became ill and died. Though it has never been proven, it has been suspected that Ieyasu had him poisoned, since with his Toyotomi sympathies, he could have been a threat to Ieyasu's new government.

For siding with Ieyasu in the campaign against Uesugi Kagekatsu, Maeda Toshinaga, son of the tairô member Maeda Toshiie (who had died in 1599) was given the fief taken from his brother, Takamasa. The latter had favoured his late father and sided with the loyalists, so was deposed. By backing Ieyasu, Toshinaga became the most wealthy daimyô in all Japan after Ieyasu himself, with a total income of 1,250,000 koku.

Two classes of feudal lords were established, the fudai daimyô, and the tozama daimyô. The fudai, numbering 176, were those who had been loyal before the battle, while the 86 tozama were those whose loyalty had been secured only thereafter.

By the time the Toyotomi were finally put down, in 1615, Ieyasu was no longer shôgun. He had achieved his goal of Tokugawa rule and unified the nation, and in 1605 he retired. His son, Hidetada, forgiven for the Ueda Castle debâcle during the Sekigahara campaign, was given the title.

THE CAMPAIGN
IN RETROSPECT

Although both sides had been preparing for war for months, the selection of the battlefield was a spur-of-the-moment decision. While Mitsunari had been certain that his position on the high ground would give him the advantage, he could not have foreseen the virtual – if not actual – defection of over a third of his forces.

The battle was really a contest between the Tokugawa war machine – a cohesive force of loyal vassals and allies – and the disjointed and quarrelsome Mitsunari coalition of rival lords.

One fact that the battle clearly demonstrates is the high quality of the discipline and training of both armies. In pitch darkness during a terrible storm they were able to maintain cohesion, manoeuvre, and even deploy for battle and build defenses.

It is a favourite pastime among Japanese historians to speculate on the outcome of the battle had the Môri and Kobayakawa divisions remained true to their pledge with the Western Army. For Ieyasu, their betrayal was serendipitous, as he was in a dangerous position at the start of the battle.

Ieyasu was not the kind of general to allow himself to be trapped by a larger force ensconced in good defensive positions on high ground. For all his foresight and rapidity of movement, he had positioned himself in a valley, with the roads leading into it occupied by the enemy and any retreat likely to be cut off by hostile troops. One can only speculate at what he might have done had he not been aware of the planned defections. Would he have gone to Sekigahara in the first place? Looking at the map, it is doubtful that he could have gone anywhere else, so that much seems academic. He had to take Sawayama Castle to eliminate Mitsunari's base of operations, and he needed to regain Osaka Castle from Môri Terumoto. The only way to get there was down the narrow waist of Honshû, and Sekigahara was in his way.

Mitsunari too was drawn to Sekigahara as the best option available. Although he didn't choose the site, he prepared admirably for a frontal assault. Ironically, it was the greater Môri clan, who either didn't fight or fought for the other side, who chose the site for him. It was Kobayakawa Hideaki, a Môri clan affiliate, who set his camp up on Mount Matsuo and Môri Hidemoto, Kikkawa Hiroie, and Ankokuji Ekei who set their positions on the eastern flank of Mount Nangû; this well before Ieyasu was near.

Folding helmets were often worn with folding armours. This model folds almost flat, to the depth of one lame (perhaps as little as 1.5 ins.). The fastener, a latch at the top, is usually connected to the half-hoop that hangs behind the helmet 'bowl'. When the hoop is up and latched, the bowl of the helmet retains its hemispherical shape. (Nagakute Battlefield Museum)

It is a supreme irony that Ankokuji Ekei, Ishida Mitsunari's agent in the camp of the Môri clan, who was responsible for bringing so many of that clan into the Western fold (and thereby inadvertently bringing about their fall), failed to bring his own division into engagement with the enemy when the moment was right. Instead, he fled, his command routed, and he was captured and executed.

Indeed, a great deal of martial potential was wasted. There simply wasn't decent land available for both armies to be fully deployed, for one thing. For another, only a part of the Western Army was directly involved in combat, while virtually all of Ieyasu's available forces – save the 36,000 Hidetada had at Ueno Castle – were engaged. There were also another 30,000 of Mitsunari's men involved futilely in the sieges at Otsu and Tanabe.

Another major reason for the defeat of the Western forces aside from the defections (though a connected factor) was the mettle and nature of the two commanders-in-chief. The Eastern Army had Tokugawa Ieyasu in undisputed command of his forces. He was the supreme commander-in-chief for vassal and ally alike; his orders were carried out without hesitation. Ishida Mitsunari, as much as he wanted to, was simply unable and perhaps unfit to fill that role. Many daimyô participating in the battle were doing so out of loyalty not to Mitsunari, but to the heir of Toyotomi Hideyoshi. They were more likely to listen to their own clan counsellors, and follow their own plans (as Shimazu Yoshihiro did) than take commands from someone they saw as a scheming politician dabbling in military affairs. In this, they did a disservice to their cause, because by failing to present a unified front they allowed themselves to be defeated and taken piecemeal. Additionally, Mitsunari was greatly detested by many in the Eastern camp, and with him as the principle figure in the Western Army, he was little more than a magnet to attract the hatred of the East.

THE BATTLEFIELD TODAY

Thanks to the convenient train network in Japan, the battlefield is easy to get to. The Sekigahara station is on the Tôkaidô Line, 30 minutes from Gifu and an hour from Nagoya. By road, the Meishin Highway is the new Tôkaidô, cutting through the town; the Nakasendô is still there, though that is now a highway too. Sekigahara is still a small town, and besides schools and a few small factories, the largest single institution seems to be a phenomenally gaudy pachinko parlour some ten minutes' walk from the station.

The battlefield itself is now covered by rice paddies and the slowly spreading sprawl of Sekigahara. The town itself is neither urban nor truly rural.

A park in the centre of the town marks the spot of the final Tokugawa camp, and in it is a raised area that was the actual site where he and his commanders sat to view the heads of the enemy that had been taken in battle. Oddly, the park has little of the air of a battlefield monument about it; more a place for picnics, concerts in the park and civic festivities. Across the street, however, is the Sekigahara Public Museum. Therein may be found arms and armour, exhibits relating to the battle, documents, books and a great many maps.

There are suggested walks that between them take in most of the battlefield sites, though following all of them would take the better part of two days.

The place where the final battle was decided, the kessen-ba, is in the middle of the rice paddies, a short walk from the highway that has replaced the old Nakasendô. The site is marked by a stone obelisk, a small sign, several banners bearing the crests of samurai clans that fought there and an outhouse.

Mount Sasao, the mountain that held Ishida's camp, has a path up one side and down the other, making it easy to scale. From its peak, one can view the entire valley, and get an idea of how the battle was actually fought.

If one has the stamina to get there and make the climb, Mount Matsuo, on the valley's other side and taller than Mount Sasao, provides a better overlook of the valley. From here, one can see the field through the eyes of Kobayakawa Hideaki.

ABOVE RIGHT *The spot where Ieyasu set up his final camp to view heads is now the centre of a municipal park in the city of Sekigahara. It was built into a mound by the lord of the Sekigahara fief in 1841 on the orders of his Edo masters.*

RIGHT *Although the city of Sekigahara has far outgrown its boundaries of 1600, and in so doing swallowed up a great portion of the battlefield, some areas still look much as they must have when thousands of armoured troops slogged through the mud. On the right in the distance is the kessenba, where the final struggle played out.*

A short taxi-ride from the station (or a further hike from the battlefield) is Sekigahara Warland, a theme-park of sorts. Several dozen life-size plaster statues of armoured samurai show vignettes of the battle. These statues are best viewed from a distance, as the vision of the designers was better than their ability to execute that vision. However, it is interesting.

The best thing about Sekigahara Warland is the arms and armour museum on the second floor of the gatehouse. On display are some three dozen or more full suits and many more helmets. It is an excellent cross-section of the styles of armour common (and some not-so-common) at the end of the 16th century. The sad fact is that the execution of the display is far inferior to the quality of the goods therein; a single fluorescent strip down the centre of the ceiling reflects off the glass of the display cases, so the exhibits are all in shadow.

Nearer to the station is the shrine built in honour of the heads of Western samurai slain in the battle.

This simple monument marks the site of the fiercest fighting of the battle. Called the kessenba, it was the place at which the battle was decided. The crests on the banners are those of Ieyasu (right) and Mitsunari (left).

CHRONOLOGY

Due to the oddities of the historical calendar used in Japan (the year 1599 repeated the month of March, for one thing), Sekigahara is listed in every book in Japan as having occurred on 15 September. On the modern Western calendar, that date is given as 21 October. It is enormously difficult to reconcile different dates for the same event in English publications, so the dates on this chronology (listed according to the Western calendar) follow the dates given for the events in Japanese history books, using 21 October to mean 15 September.

1598

15 September – Hideyoshi dies, aged 72, in Fushimi Castle.

1599

April – Maeda Toshiie dies in Osaka. Kuroda Nagamasa, Katô Kiyomasa and others plan to attack Ishida Mitsunari, who flees to Ieyasu in Fushimi Castle, and a few days later returns to Sawayama Castle.

28 October – Ieyasu relocates from Fushimi Castle to Osaka Castle.

1600

7 May – Ieyasu sends Uesugi Kagekatsu a letter demanding an explanation for his military build-up, and an apology.

8 June – Ieyasu receives the reply. In his anger, he calls for all the daimyô to gather to punish the Uesugi.

12 July – The daimyô meet in Osaka, and Ieyasu plans an expedition to subjugate Uesugi Kagekatsu in Aizu.

22 July – Ieyasu's generals leave Osaka Castle. Date Masamune leaves Fushimi Castle for his home north of Aizu. Môgami Yoshimitsu, Satake Yoshinobu and Nanbu Toshinao also head for their home provinces.

24 July – Ieyasu leaves Osaka Castle.

26 July – Ieyasu leaves Fushimi Castle after meeting with Torii Mototada.

16 August – Ishida Mitsunari meets Otani Yoshitsugu, who is on his way to Aizu, invites him to Sawayama, and lays plans to destroy Ieyasu.

17 August – Ankokuji Ekei, Otani Yoshitsugu, Ishida Mitsunari and Mashita Nagamori meet in Sawayama and agree to invite Môri Terumoto to be commander-in-chief. Nagamori secretly sends word to Ieyasu about the meeting and the outcome.

22 August – Môri Terumoto enters Osaka Castle and assumes the mantle of leadership of the Western Army and protectorship of Toyotomi Hideyori. Maeda Munehisa, Nagatsuka Masaie and Mashita Nagamori issue the letter of 13 complaints, and call for a general campaign to quash Ieyasu.

25 August – Otani Yoshitsugu gets support for the West from Sanada Masayuki and Yukimura.

27 August – Fushimi Castle is attacked.

29 August – Ieyasu arrives in Oyama and establishes a base. The next day he calls a council to discuss matters taking place in the West.

6 September – The Western Army captures Fushimi Castle. Torii Mototada commits suicide.

7 September – Maeda Toshinaga (for the East) attacks his own brother, Toshimasa, and lays siege to Daishôji Castle. The garrison commander, Yamaguchi Munenaga, commits suicide.

10 September – Ieyasu returns to Edo Castle from Oyama.

15 September – Mitsunari enters Ogaki Castle.

27 September – Fukushima Masanori, Ikeda Terumasa and others leave Kiyosu to take Gifu Castle.

28 September – The vanguard of the Eastern Army lays siege to Oda Hidenobu in Gifu Castle.

Hidenobu sent to Kôyasan under guard.

29 September – Nabeshima Naoshige and others of the Western Army lay siege to Matsuoka Castle. The 'Tôkaidô Corps' of the Eastern Army occupies the heights of Akasaka, confronting Ôgaki Castle. Tokugawa Hidetada and his 'Nakasendô Corps' head towards Mino.

30 September – Môri Hidemoto lays siege to Annotsu Castle.

1 October – Mitsunari returns to Sawayama Castle from Ogaki, urges Môri Terumoto to come up.

7 October – Ieyasu leaves Edo at the head of a 30,000 man army. Hidetada reaches Karuizawa in Mino.

9 October – Hidetada reaches Komoro, and, against his father's orders, diverts his forces toward Ueda.

12 October – Ieyasu reaches Shimada in Suruga. Hidetada makes camp in the village of Sometani to lay siege to Sanada Masayuki in Ueda Castle.

13 October – Ieyasu reaches Nakaizumi in Tôtômi. Môri Hidemoto and Kikkawa Hiroie enter Mino and make camp near Mount Nangû. Loyalists Môri Motoyasu, Tachibana Muneshige and Tsukushi Hirokado lay siege to Otsu Castle, held for Ieyasu by Kyôgoku Takatsugu.

14 October – Ieyasu, on the march in Suruga, receives a secret messenger from Kobayakawa Hideaki, offering support.

16 October – Hidetada breaks off the siege of Ueda Castle and turns again toward Mino.

Helmets of 72 plates were the prerogative of samurai of wealth. Such kabuto were more tours-de-force for the armourer than protection, however. Helmets of 120 plates were also made, but these were mere show-pieces for the wealthy. Note the unusually complicated crest holder just above the visor. (Yoroi no Kôzan-dô)

This section of a battle
screen is supposed to indicate
a vignette from the battle,
but the armour is anachro-
nistically old. It is a
classical Edo period (1600-
1868) romantic view of the
battle. (Sekigahara Warland)

19 October – Ieyasu enters Gifu.
Hosokawa Yûsai surrenders
Tanabe Castle.

20 October

Noon – Ieyasu enters Akasaka.
Eastern and Western forces are
involved in a skirmish beside
the Kuisegawa, near Akasaka.

7.00 pm – The Western Army
sets out for Sekigahara
from Ôgaki Castle.

21 OCTOBER – THE BATTLE OF SEKIGAHARA

Midnight – Ieyasu is notified of
Ishida Mitsunari's movement.
Ieyasu plans to march to
Sekigahara as well.

2.00 am – Despite blinding rain,
the Western Army begins to
take positions on the high
ground and straddling the
roads. The Eastern Army sets
out from Akasaka, with
Fukushima Masanori leading.

4.30 am – Both armies are in

place. Fog prevents clear
appraisal of enemy positions.
Fukushima's vanguard acciden-
tally contacts Ukita's forces
and withdraws.

8.00 am – Fog lifts. Battle begins
with Ii Naomasa's division
attacking Ukita Hideie.
Fushima Masanori's division
joins Ii's in the attack. Several
Eastern generals make direct
attacks on Mitsunari's first
line. Ieyasu moves forward.

10.00 am – Behind Mount Nangû,
Tokugawa vassal Asano
Yukinaga attacks Natsuka
Masaie. Otani Yoshitsugu's
division engages Kyôgoku
Takatomo. Ukita Hideie and
Konishi Yukinaga are in heated
combat with Eastern forces.

11.00 am – Ieyasu moves forward
again. Mitsunari is thwarted as
first the Shimazu, then the
Môri and then the Kobayakawa
fail to move as instructed.

Noon – Kobayakawa Hideaki
finally leaves his position on

Mount Sasao and attacks Ôtani Yoshitsugu, his erstwhile ally, prompting a series of defections. Ôtani orders himself killed. Konishi Yukinaga and Ukita Hideie are forced to flee into the mountains, their forces crushed. The Shimazu are hard-pressed by Ii Naomasa.

1.00 pm – Shimazu Toyohisa is killed, and Shimazu Yoshihiro leads remaining troops in retreat south around Mount Nangû. Mitsunari flees.

2.00 pm – Ieyasu declares victory and prepares to receive his commanders and view the heads of the slain enemy.

3.00 pm – Kobayakawa Hideaki presents himself to Ieyasu, who expresses gratitude. Hidetada arrives.

22 October – The Eastern Army – principally defecting units – led by Kobayakawa Hideaki lays siege to Sawayama Castle.

23 October – Sawayama falls; its commanders commit suicide. Ogaki Castle's defenders surrender.

25 October – Konishi Yukinaga is found hiding on Mount Ibuki.

26 October – Ieyasu enters Otsu Castle.

27 October – Ishida Mitsunari is found hiding on Mount Ibuki.

29 October – Ankokuji Ekei is captured in Kyôto.

30 October – Môri Terumoto withdraws from the Osaka Castle.

2 November – Ieyasu occupies the Osaka Castle.

5 November – Ikeda Terumasa defeats Natsuka Masaie in Mizoguchi Castle. Masaie commits suicide. Uesugi Kagekatsu learns of the defeat of the Western Army, and withdraws his forces. The 'Sekigahara campaign' officially ends.

6 November – Konishi Yukinaga, Ankokuji Ekei and Ishida Mitsunari are beheaded at Kyôto's Rokujô-ga-hara execution grounds.

A GUIDE TO
FURTHER READING

Sekigahara is unfortunately scarcely covered in English. It usually gets but a paragraph or two in history books, and sometimes as much as a few pages in a book on Japanese history. It is not surprising, therefore, that most of the sources are in Japanese.

Bryant, Anthony J., Samurai 1550-1600, Osprey Warrior Series, No. 7, Osprey, London, 1994. The seventh volume in the Warrior Series presents the typical samurai; these were the men who fought at Sekigahara.

Bryant, Anthony J., The Samurai, Osprey Élite Series, No. 23, Osprey, London, 1994.

Kadokawa Editorial Office (Eds.), Nihon Shi Tanbô: Sekigahara to Ôsaka no Jin [Inquiry into Japanese History: Sekigahara and the Ôsaka Siege], Kadokawa Shoten, Tokyo, 1983.

Ôda Takeo (Ed.), Sekigahara no Tatakai [The Battle of Sekigahara], Rekishi Gunzô Series, No. 4, Gakushû Kenkyû Sha, Tokyo, 1987. Now over 35 volumes in length, the irregularly-published 'Gakken' series on history

This participant in an annual festival in northern Japan wears full armour typical of the mounted samurai. In battle he would probably be carrying a lance as well. Note the banner attached to his back.

has focused on individuals (Nobunaga, Hideyoshi, Ieyasu), on campaigns (Onin War, Sekigahara) and even on foreign topics (China's Age of Battles, the Korean campaign).

Sadler, A.L., The Maker of Modern Japan, George Allen & Unwin Co., London, 1937. Sadler's biography of Tokugawa Ieyasu is very stilted, but excellent nevertheless. It is reprinted in paperback by Charles E. Tuttle, of Rutland, Vermont and Tokyo.

Sansom, G., A History of Japan 1334–1615, Stanford University Press, Stanford, CA, 1961. This is the second book in Sansom's three-volume history of Japan. Dr. Sansom describes at length the machinations before Sekigahara, and in appendices provides speculative (albeit very dated) information on the armies' make-up.

Soda Yasunori and Gotô Tsutomu, Sengoku Gassen Gaido [Warring States Battle Guide], Shinkigensha, Tokyo, 1993.

Tamaru Nobuyuki (ED.), Senryaku, Senjutsu, Heiki: Nihon Sengoku Hen [Strategy, Tactics, Weapons: Japanese Age of Battles Edition], Graphic Rekishi Series, Gakushû Kenkyûsha, Tokyo, 1994.

Tanaka Mitsuyoshi (Ed.), Bôryaku! Sekigahara kara Osaka no Jin e [Plots! From Sekigahara to the Osaka Siege], Rekishi Dokuhon [History Reader], December, 1985. Rekishi Dokuhon is a wonderful historical journal. It focuses on a particular topic each month, and the articles, by various historians, provide valuable and occasionally controversial information.

Turnbull, S., Battles of the Samurai, Arms and Armour Press, London, 1987. Just about anything by Stephen Turnbull is worth a read, but this book is especially useful as it concentrates on several famous encounters that are virtually ignored in English books.

Turnbull, S., The Samurai, Macmillan Publishing, New York City, 1977. Turnbull's most impressive book, this provides an overall history and look at Japan. Sekigahara is treated well, and given ample coverage.

INDEX

(References to illustrations are shown in **bold**)

COMPANION SERIES FROM OSPREY

MEN-AT-ARMS

An unrivalled source of information on the organisation, uniforms and equipment of the world's fighting men, past and present. The series covers hundreds of subjects spanning 5,000 years of history. Each 48-page book includes concise texts packed with specific information, some 40 photos, maps and diagrams, and eight colour plates of uniformed figures.

ELITE

Detailed information on the uniforms and insignia of the world's most famous military forces. Each 64-page book contains some 50 photographs and diagrams, and 12 pages of full-colour artwork.

NEW VANGUARD

Comprehensive histories of the design, development and operational use of the world's armoured vehicles and artillery. Each 48-page book contains eight pages of full-colour artwork including a detailed cutaway.

WARRIOR

Definitive analysis of the armour, weapons, tactics and motivation of the fighting men of history. Each 64-page book contains cutaways and exploded artwork of the warrior's weapons and armour.

ORDER OF BATTLE

The most detailed information ever published on the units which fought history's great battles. Each 96-page book contains comprehensive organisation diagrams supported by ultra-detailed colour maps. Each title also includes a large fold-out base map.

AIRCRAFT OF THE ACES

Focuses exclusively on the elite pilots of major air campaigns, and includes unique interviews with surviving aces sourced specifically or each volume. Each 96-page volume contains up to 40 specially commissioned artworks, unit listings, new scale plans and the best archival photography available.

COMBAT AIRCRAFT

Technical information from the world's leading aviation writers on the aircraft types flown. Each 96-page volume contains up to 40 specially commissioned artworks, unit listings, new scale plans and the best archival photography available.